At Home with History:

The Untold Secrets of Greater Vancouver's Heritage Homes

At Home with History:

The Untold Secrets of Greater Vancouver's Heritage Homes

Eve Lazarus

ANVIL PRESS | VANCOUVER

At Home with History: The Untold Secrets of Greater Vancouver's Heritage Homes
Copyright © 2007 by Eve Lazarus

Anvil Press Inc.
P.O. Box 3008, Main Post Office
Vancouver, B.C. V6B 3X5 CANADA
www.anvilpress.com

LIBRARY AND ARCHIVES CANADA CATALOGUING IN PUBLICATION

Lazarus, Eve
    At home with history : the untold secrets of Greater Vancouver's heritage homes / Eve Lazarus.

Includes bibliographical references and index.
ISBN 978-1-895636-80-2

    1. Historic buildings—British Columbia—Vancouver.   2. Dwellings—British Columbia—Vancouver—History.   3. Vancouver (B.C.)—History.
    I. Title.

FC3847.7.L39 2007   971.1'33   C2007-901758-4

The author and publisher assert that the information contained in this book is true and complete to the best of their knowledge. The author and publisher disclaim any liability in connection with the use of this information. All reasonable efforts have been made to locate the copyright holder of source material wherever possible. The publisher would be pleased to have any errors or omissions brought to its attention.

Printed and bound in Canada
Cover design: Typesmith Design
Interior design & typesetting: HeimatHouse

Represented in Canada by the Literary Press Group
Distributed by the University of Toronto Press

The publisher gratefully acknowledges the financial assistance of the Canada Council for the Arts, the Book Publishing Industry Development Program (BPIDP), and the Province of British Columbia through the B.C. Arts Council and the Book Publishing Tax Credit.

for Mike,
Mark,
Megan and Matthew

ACKNOWLEDGEMENTS

When I started collecting and documenting stories of various houses in Greater Vancouver, it was quickly apparent that they needed a historical context, and I needed a crash course in history. Fortunately, British Columbia has a prolific and passionate group of authors. Many I've listed in the bibliography at the back of the book, but some names just kept coming up over and over again: Chuck Davis, Michael Kluckner, John Atkin, Donald Luxton, Jim Wolf, Janet Bingham, and *The Vancouver Sun*'s John Mackie.

Chuck Davis, a walking encyclopedia when it comes to local history, was kind enough to look over my manuscript and save me from some historical blunders. James Johnstone, an amazingly thorough home history researcher, gave me research tips, loaned me books, shared information, took me on a walking tour of Strathcona, and gave me a ton of encouragement. Thanks also to Donald Luxton, Raymond Culos and Jim Wolf who gave me their time and expert knowledge.

While much of the research for this book came from city directories, heritage inventories, past heritage house tours, old newspapers, the Vancouver City Hall's Heritage Group, and, wherever possible, personal interviews, it's unlikely that any historical project could be completed without the diverse resources and staff at the City of Vancouver Archives and the Vancouver Public Library's Special Collections and History and Government Divisions. Special thanks to the CVA's Megan Schlase and the many times she patiently helped me find answers, as did Andrew Martin at Special Collections. Help also came from Daien Ide at the North Vancouver Museum & Archives, Kobi Howard at Langley Centennial Museum, Kathy Bossort at Delta Museum and Archives, and Wendy Turnbull at the New Westminster Public Library.

Sincere thanks to the dozens of homeowners and past and current residents who shared their personal stories with me, loaned me photos, and let me into their houses. You'll meet them in the pages of this book.

And, of course, there's the team at Anvil Press. I'm extremely grateful to publisher Brian Kaufman for sharing my enthusiasm for this project, to Kate Lancaster for wrestling it into shape, and to Karen Green for getting the word out.

—E.L.

Contents

Preface

A house has a genealogy, much like a person, and comes alive through the human interest stories and mysteries that took place inside its walls. Over time, changes inevitably occur; but through it all, the house remains a central fixture and the structure for the stories that follow.

It might start with a scratch on a wall, initials carved in the basement, or a decades-old electricity bill that fell out from behind the furnace. Once you've lived in an older house, it's easy to become curious, not only about its architectural details, but also about the lives of the people who once slept under your roof.

I first became obsessed with home histories in 2002. While planning a trip back to Australia, I discovered a 1970 biography about my aunt Joan Rosanove. The book gave the address of the house where my father was born in a country town northwest of Melbourne. One intriguing paragraph described my father's mother, Ruby, who died years before I was born. Ruby was more than a little eccentric, which explains some of the odder features of her house.

The house was an old Victorian painted mud yellow, sitting behind a picket fence painted the same colour. Cast-iron lacework decorated the front of the house and ran along a verandah supported by fluted iron pillars. The current owners let me look around, and I filled them in on thirty years of their home's social history. They'd raised five children in the house, and thanks to the book and Ruby, I was able to solve their twenty-year mystery as to why there were a number of doors that led nowhere. Apparently, as each of Ruby's eight children moved away, she had their bedrooms lopped off the house. Why, no one really knows.

Around the same time, I met James Johnstone. James is a house detective in Vancouver who researches and writes home histories filled with information about past residents. I also spoke to other home historians across the country and interviewed past and current residents of heritage homes to document as much as possible of the social history behind heritage homes in Greater Vancouver.

Research for the book led me in dozens of different directions. It was important to me that the stories were about houses that still stood. Sometimes I'd come across a great story only to find that the house was long gone. Other times I'd come across what seemed a particularly interesting house only to find that nothing out of the ordinary ever took place there. Wherever possible, I've tried to find people who could tell me their own stories.

Through my research, I found and interviewed a maid who worked at one of Vancouver's wealthiest homes in the '30s and a policeman who walked the Eastside beat during the Depression. They both had vivid memories of some of the more notable homes and neighbourhoods described in this book. I talked with the son of a rum runner and the son of an architect who designed homes for the rich. The grandsons of both Yip Sang and Alvo von Alvensleben talked to me about their ancestors—two men who lived in Vancouver at the turn of the twentieth century, but who couldn't have been more different. Others throughout the book generously gave me insights into the people, culture, politics, and houses of the past. For me, it was these personal stories that made the houses and neighbourhoods of Greater Vancouver's history come alive.

In researching and writing this book, I came to believe that we are only temporary custodians of the houses in which we live and part of a chain in the ongoing narrative of the house. And I'm convinced that the social history of a house is every bit as important as its architectural history in preserving buildings for future generations.

Both at the provincial and the federal level, and increasingly at the municipal level, governments are also coming around to this point of view.

When the City of Vancouver introduced the Heritage Register in 1986, the foremost concern was saving buildings deemed architecturally important. The register identified prominent Shaughnessy houses such as Glen Brae and Hycroft, West End houses that had escaped the apartment blitz of the 1950s, such as Roedde House on Barclay Street and the Thomas Fee House on Broughton Street, as well as various churches, schools, and public buildings in different areas of the city. Not surprisingly, most of these houses and buildings are rather grand and all built before 1940.

While the Heritage Register was a huge step in preserving Vancouver's architectural history, the City recognizes a pressing need to document and preserve more recent buildings and, more importantly, to determine cultural and social values that go beyond the four walls and reflect our growth as a city. In 2007, the city announced it would spend $750,000 over three years to upgrade the register. It's a huge change in thinking, and now instead of being a negative, the whole idea of heritage and social history is appealing to both developers and governments alike.

Instead of seeing value only in the land beneath an older building, developers now see heritage as something that adds spice to projects, lets them pick up some financial incentives from the City, and adds caché when it comes to marketing and later reselling the property.

Nationally, historicplaces.ca, an online searchable database, is an initiative started by the federal government in 1999, with input from the provincial and territorial governments, to identify properties with heritage value. By 2007, the register had about three thousand historic place listings and expects this to grow to more than seventeen thousand over the next few years. It includes everything from private residences and commercial buildings, to structures like barns and silos. While architecture is important, the statement of significance used to compile the listings has three sections: historic place, heritage value, and character-defining elements. The idea is to explain why a historic place is important to the community from a social and cultural, as well as an architectural, perspective.

Another emerging term is "vernacular heritage." This confusing title was the theme for Vancouver Heritage Week 2007. Described as architecture without architects, the idea is that ordinary and everyday houses reflect our culture and ethnic diversity over a certain period of time. Jim Wolf, heritage planner for the City of Burnaby, says that when Burnaby's first heritage program began, the focus was on outstanding architect-designed mansions of the wealthy. But it ignored the heritage of Burnaby's working-class pioneers. Wolf calls these threatened heritage bungalows "bulldozer bait."

It's encouraging that governments are concerned with preserving examples of our architectural history: the elegant, the interesting, and even the plain awful. But it's equally heartening that they are now as concerned with preserving buildings because of their rich social history—a history that goes well beyond the four walls of a house.

When James Johnstone has a spare moment, he spends it researching what he calls his "orphan" houses. These are mostly small and neglected and often destined for demolition. Many are in his East End neighbourhood. Johnstone believes that if he can research a house's history and show it has a story, there's a chance that those houses may be saved.

I hope he's right.

—Eve Lazarus, North Vancouver, April 2007

Introduction

Old houses have stories. It doesn't matter whether they are small cottages or multi-million dollar mansions. Over the years they may have housed bootlegging joints or secret rooms, or murders, or ghosts. More importantly, the houses that still stand provide a context for the social history of Greater Vancouver and reveal secrets that would otherwise be forgotten or hidden forever.

Writer Joy Kogawa's childhood house is one such example. A modest wood-framed bungalow in South Vancouver's Marpole, it's about a fifteen-minute drive south of downtown Vancouver, just off Granville Street. There's nothing really architecturally significant about it except that it's one of the few original houses that remain in the neighbourhood. What makes it of great historical importance and worth preserving is the house's social history.

1450 West Sixty-fourth Avenue figures prominently in Kogawa's classic novel *Obasan*, considered one of the one hundred most important Canadian books ever written. The house is a physical reminder of the time when twenty two thousand Japanese-Canadians—fishermen, miners, merchants, and foresters—were wrenched from their homes and interned at places like Slocan, B.C. during the Second World War. It was a shocking period in Canada's history. Kogawa's house is an important monument to that time.

Obasan tells the story of the Japanese internment through the eyes of six-year-old Naomi Nakane who, in 1942, had her family ripped apart by the war. "The house, if I must remember it today, was large and beautiful. It's still there on West 64th Avenue in Vancouver. Phone Langara 0938-R. I looked it up once in the November 1941 inch-thick Vancouver telephone directory. I wrote to the people who lived there and asked if they would ever consider selling the house, but they never replied. I don't know their names. I don't know what they've done to the house. It used to have a hedge and rose bushes and flowers and cactus plants lining the sidewalk, and the front iron gate had a squeeze latch. The backyard had a sand box and an apple tree and a swing, and I could dangle by my knees from a branch thicker than my father's arms," writes Kogawa in *Obasan*.

In 2003, Kogawa, who now lives in Toronto, drove past the old house while on a trip to Vancouver. She was stunned to find that it was for sale. "But the asking price was out of sight, over five hundred thousand dollars," she told a *Vancouver Sun* reporter at the time. "Still it was amazing that the house was still there, when all around it, the old houses were gone and replaced with new ones."

When it looked like the new owner was set to demolish the old house, Chris Kurata, a Toronto lawyer and writer, formed the Joy Kogawa Homestead Committee and with a growing membership of concerned citizens, joined with the Land Conservancy to save the house from demolition.

While huge numbers of perfectly solid heritage houses have been torn down all over Vancouver, replaced by Vancouver specials or monster houses or parking lots or subsidized government housing, those that remain form an important part of the city's early history. For this book, dozens of people have shared stories about their homes and what it was like growing up in different parts of Greater Vancouver.

The story starts with the East End, now known as Strathcona, the city's oldest neighbourhood. Through the residents, these houses tell the story of immigration and survival in early Vancouver. The houses sheltered British working class immigrants, which over time changed to Japanese, Jewish, Russian, Italian, and Chinese. Among some of the many notable people that once lived in the area are writers Paul Yee and Wayson Choy. Nora Hendrix lived there in the 1940s and her grandson, rocker Jimi Hendrix was a frequent visitor. A young and up-and-coming boxer from the neighbourhood, Phil Palmer, fought forty-one professional fights at Madison Square Gardens.

In the 1930s, it was common to see East End families scrape through the Depression by selling cheap booze. One Italian woman remembers her family of six supplementing their meagre income by selling shots of home-made liquor. Later, they sold the house to a major bootlegger who used the garage as a distribution centre. Today that same garage is a studio for Brian Dedora, a master gilder.

A new owner to Strathcona realized that her home was once a Chinese sausage factory after she found a slew of equipment in her basement: grinding machines, iceboxes with glass fronts, hooks, and wooden handles with spikes that once moved big slabs of meat around.

Another family, while renovating their Princess Street home, found a mix of artefacts hidden behind the walls. They uncovered Chinese and Russian newspapers, picture postcards, whisky bottles, a cigarette case, and condoms. Old-timers believe that the house has, at different times, been a brothel, a high-end bootlegging joint, and a rooming house.

On the west side of town, Depression-proof mansions, hunting lodges, and cabarets sprung up, built on the proceeds of bootlegging to thirsty Americans during the thirteen years of Prohibition. Some west-side houses were the homes of local law enforcers, many of whom weren't very different from the criminals they threw in jail.

A large Kerrisdale house, now the home of Crofton House School, was once owned by Alvo von Alvensleben, the larger-than-life son of a German count who brought millions of dollars into Vancouver in the early years of the Twentieth Century. Rumour had it that he was a German spy with a secret radio room and tunnels in his houses. To this day, these homes bear names like "Alien Acres" and "Spy House."

New Westminster was once the capital of British Columbia, and although homes predating the Nineteenth Century are rare in other parts of Vancouver, New Westminster still has an abundance of Queen-Anne mansions, quaint cottages, and sturdy Georgian, Tudor Revival, and Arts and Crafts houses. These houses have over a century worth of stories to share.

After the focus of development began to shift from New Westminster to Vancouver, the West End became home to the rich, and fabulous mansions sprung up only to turn into boarding houses and, later still, apartment buildings during the building boom of the 1950s. Some escaped demolition and tell the tale of the West End, once the desired place to live before the emergence of Shaughnessy Heights.

The Canadian Pacific Railway played a huge role in shaping early Vancouver, first at Mount Pleasant and later in Shaughnessy Heights. The names of many of its early employees, Abbott, Hamilton, Marguerite, Marpole, Shaughnessy, Salsbury, Nanton, and many more, live on in the names of our streets and suburbs.

Shaughnessy, the enclave of the rich, has had its share of scandals such as the infamous and unsolved Janet Smith murder that took place in 1924 and rocked the city. But murder, of course, has no boundaries, and sensational crimes have occurred in every area, for all sorts of reasons and cut across all income groups. Perhaps it's some of these victims who wander the halls of haunted houses; but others, such as the spirit who haunts the Burnaby Art Gallery, is believed to be a former resident, Grace Ceperley. Ghosts, it seems, don't discriminate where or whom they haunt.

And not to be forgotten are the Chinese. They played an incredibly important part in the development of our city and flourished in the face of decades of racism and outright cruelty. It was the Chinese who organized the residents of the East End and Chinatown and who, when City Hall tried to demolish the houses, fought for and ultimately saved Strathcona.

For those wanting to unlock the secrets of their own home's history, the last chapter of

the book is designed as a "how-to" guide that helps navigate through the different docu-
ments and information sources available, and provides information on where to find
them. There's nothing particularly straightforward about home research, but the finds
are immensely rewarding.

Chapter I

STRATHCONA: VANCOUVER'S ORIGINAL EAST END

Maria Piovesan raced through the house searching for her daughter. "The police are coming Gilda, I have to go," she whispered in Italian. The older woman shot out the back reluctantly leaving the twelve-year-old to answer the front door. Two burly detectives stood there, and one asked the child if her mother was at home. "She just went out," answered Gilda. "Then you'll have to show us through the house," he said. The detectives followed Gilda into the kitchen, opened a cupboard door and then had a look in the sitting room. Finally, their boots echoed on the fir floors and up the stairs to the four bedrooms above. The detective pointed to the master bedroom. "You wouldn't have anything in here would you?" he asked her. Gilda paled and shook her long dark braids. "No," she said. The policemen glanced around once more, then, climbed down the stairs and left.

Had the policemen looked a little closer, they would have found liquor stored in Maria and Adam Piovesan's bedroom closet. At **446 Union Street**, and in many houses in the East End of the 1930s, bootlegging was often the only way to sustain life through the tough years of the Depression.

BOOTLEGGERS AND BROTHELS

In the 20s and 30s, the Italians called Strathcona Treviso, a province in Italy from where many of the Italians in the area originated. And Union Street was called the "mile of vice" for the bootleggers and brothels that swarmed the area. Yet the bootlegging joints were mostly family-run, home-based businesses, and the prostitution evolved out of a strong sense of self-preservation.

Raymond Culos grew up in the East End. Both sets of grandparents lived on Union

Street, and from 1913 the Culoses lived at 748 Union Street. Raymond Culos lived in the house from his birth in 1936 until he turned sixteen. Culos has written three books on the Italians in Vancouver and he remembers Strathcona as a warm and loving community. Grapes and wine, he says, are a tradition with the Italians, and one they continued when they moved to this country. Prohibition was long over, and if someone wanted a drink, they could visit a bar. It was mainly after hours and on Sundays when the bars were shut that people would visit Union Street. This small-time bootlegging, says Culos, started innocently enough. Families sold wine to their boarders to cover the costs, especially during the Depression. "There was lots of wine being made and the non-Italians, many of whom were on the police force, I might add, started to discover this was available and that's how it grew," he says. "These single men would have to pay for the wine because otherwise it made no sense economically."

And bootlegging was a stressful existence. Raids were commonplace, and Maria had already notched up a three hundred dollar fine—a fortune in those days and a penalty that naturally forced the family to bootleg more liquor to pay it. Caught twice, and she went to jail. "You were always on your toes waiting for something to happen," says Gilda.

Gilda remembers a colourful crowd of customers arriving at the house by taxi: Kitty the Bitch, Gumboot Annie, Shortie the Painter, Jimmy the Corker, the local Spaniard, railway workers, and a stream of loggers from the camps. They'd enter the front door and follow the long hallway down to the kitchen at the back of the house where the Piovesans dispensed their liquor.

Adam Piovesan was a longshoreman earning between seventy and eighty cents an hour, and that was when he could get work. For a while he was a partner in Star Cabs, but the taxi company went broke during the Depression. Like scores of Italian families in the area, the Piovesans made beer and wine in the European tradition and bought rum from the government-run liquor store, which they then resold in shots. A large vat of dark beer often brewed in the basement. Gilda, the oldest of four girls, remembers scrubbing out the long-necked bottles for the home brew. Beer, rum, and wine sold for a dime, while a glass of bucaro, a wine usually made from raisins and the mash of a better wine, sold for a nickel.

In the early 1940s, the Piovesans moved to a larger house in the Grandview/Woodlands area and sold 446 Union to Wally "Blondie" Wallace, one of the bigger bootleggers in the area. Wallace operated a thriving distribution centre from the garage off a lane at the back of the house where current owner Brian Dedora, a master gilder, now makes his gilded picture frames. The two-storey Edwardian house sits close to the street, its front yard not much more than an extension of the sidewalk. Built by the Piovesans in 1930, it's a solid brick house with terracotta and ochre bricks decorating the front corners of the house.

Dedora says knowing something about its social history has given him a deeper connection to the house. "It's sort of a custodial thing, like owning an antique or a painting," he says. "I'm here to take care of it for my time."

Wallace died in the 1960s and Lucille Mars, a former Strathcona resident, remembers him fondly. "He was a hell of a nice guy," she says. She added that, ironically, his wife Nellie's second marriage was to a police officer on the dry squad.

Lucille was just a kid in the Depression. Her mother, Karolina Fedychyn, emigrated from Russia in 1912, traveling first to New York and then to Halifax and on to Vancouver with her four children in the steerage section

RECENT SHOT OF 830 UNION ST.
(LUCILLE MARS' HOUSE)
PHOTO BY JAMES JOHNSTONE

of a ship. It was the same year the Titanic went down off the coast of Newfoundland, and her ship would have sailed quite near to where the Titanic sunk. In 1920, Fedychyn was forty-eight years old when she birthed Lucille, her eleventh child, in the back of an old bootlegging shack in Gastown, helped by a woman named French Marie. Two years later, she married Anton Eletz, a worker at the Sitka Spruce Lumber Company, and they bought a two-storey Edwardian house at **830 Union Street** that sits on a narrow lot with a yellow picket fence and has a large bay window in the front.

There were always boarders in the house, and in the 1930s it wasn't uncommon to have six men sleeping in one of the three upstairs bedrooms, two each on the two double beds and two on the cots. Three of the sisters shared a bed in a room under the stairs. Like most of the people in the area, the Fedychyns bootlegged red wine and whisky to make ends meet. Lucille remembers her mother walking along Union Street in a long black skirt, white shirt, and lace up boots. She worked in a coal factory down by the Canadian National Railway station and sewed sacks in a house on East Georgia Street, charging a penny for a gunny sack and two cents for a coal sack.

By age ten, Lucille was an entrepreneur. She'd spend Sundays playing the mouth organ and tap dancing on the concrete stairs of the bank at the corner of Main and Prior streets, earning ten or fifteen cents. Sometimes she'd stop in for candy at the general store a few doors down from her house on Union Street that had a well known bootlegging enterprise in the back. Lucille would tear around the neighbourhood on a borrowed bike with her best friend Mary perched on the handlebars. After school and on weekends, she'd

Lucille Mars, 3, and Her Brother Stephen Fedychyn, 15. Taken in Front of 830 Union Street, 1923.

ride to the back of a large yellow house at the corner of Gore and Union Streets, knock on the door, and ask if there were any odd jobs. If she was lucky, one of the visiting big shots would flick her a silver dollar, or one of the whores would pay her a quarter to run an errand. Often she'd take a note and some money to the druggist on East Hastings Street, returning with a little box that she'd shake to hear the rattling sound inside.

Lucille says, "I'd say to Mary, 'I know what's in here, its dope.'" She says, "I always wanted to know what was in the little box." She found out a dozen years later at a small café by the Patricia Hotel. "I saw one of the working girls from the whorehouse, and I said, 'Excuse me, you look familiar. Did you ever work in a house on Union and Gore?' And she said, 'I sure did, honey.' I said, 'I always wanted to know what was in the little box; it sounded like grains of sugar.' And she said, 'Honey, that was pot ash. We used to wash ourselves with it—it's a disinfectant.'"

Lucille also remembers Angelo Branca, the Eastside lawyer and judge of the B.C. Supreme Court, joking with her and her friends. "He'd walk by and say, 'One day all you kids are going to go to Hollywood!'" Branca was an Italian Eastside success story. Born in 1903 to Filippo and Teresa Branca, he grew up at **343 Prior Street** with a sister, Anne, and two brothers, John and Joseph. Filippo ran the grocery store on Main Street, and he and Peter Tosi and Sam Minichiello were the three biggest importers of California grapes in the area. Raymond Culos, whose grandfather was Sam Minichiello, says the joke in the neighbourhood was that wine was a family affair. Filippo would sell the grapes to the bootleggers, his son John, a detective with the dry-squad, would arrest them, and his other son, Angelo, would get them off in court.

In 1979, Branca told Carole Itter and Daphne Marlatt, co-authors of *Opening Doors: Vancouver's East End,* that he used to represent many of the madams in the 1930s and that, overall, there was little crime in Strathcona. "There were bootlegging joints, of course, but no drugs in those days," he said. "In the early days, all the whorehouses in the city were down on this end of Main Street. Later on, the brothels became a little more distributed: there were one or two along Union Street in the two-hundred and three-hundred blocks, there were some along Gore Avenue between Prior Street and Keefer, there were some along Dunlevy."

EARLY IMMIGRATION

CBC broadcaster and author Bill Richardson can't lay claim to having a brothel or a bootlegging joint in his Dunlevy Street home, but, nevertheless, the house's former residents reflect the early history of the area.

When Richardson bought the dilapidated house at **808 Dunlevy** in 2002, he knew he was in for years of renovations. What he didn't know was that he would also become part of the story of the house. He says, "In my altruistic moments, I've said to myself that this house is like a little gift to the city because there aren't many left that are like it. I'm glad to have given it another fifty or sixty years with these repairs and taken my place in the ongoing narrative of the house."

Called a "folk Victorian," better described as a worker's cottage, Richardson's house was built in 1895 on a small lot and was originally one of four identical houses. Only two, Richardson's and the house next door at 814 Dunlevy, remain.

In the original house the main door would have opened directly into the living room. The floor plan was a simple two-up, two-down design with a kitchen extension at the back. The house had clapboard siding, fir floors, and tongue and groove fir on the interior walls and ceilings. The staircase was narrow and steep, and the small rooms easy to heat.

Richardson's house has survived fires and the whims of developers and city planners. It also tells a little of the social history of Strathcona. The original builder, John Rauch, was an American of German heritage. For the next two decades, the cottage was home to British-born families with names such as Fred and Minnie Appleyard, Edward Clough, and the Scottish-born Dougal Stewart. Vancouver city directories show some of the men worked at the Hastings Sawmill at the foot of Dunlevy Street, the Canadian Pacific Railway, and as general labourers and janitors. By 1916 more and more of the names in the directory are Chinese, with the notable exception of Dude Gaines, an African American from the U.S. who arrived with his wife Marnie in 1921. The names start to change again after the Gaines leave. There's a Polish second-hand store owner, a Norwegian boat builder, and again in the 1930s, a series of Chinese occupants who were sometimes simply listed as "Orientals." The names come full circle in this century when they are Anglo once again.

"It's fascinating knowing a little bit of the biographies of the people that were here," says Richardson. "Dude Gaines was a porter for the railway, so that meant the house was part of that whole Hogan's Alley community; and I like knowing, because I'm a deeply white, waspy person, that all these different ethnicities have been in play in the house."

In 1972, the building of the Georgia viaduct wiped out the infamous Hogan's Alley. At one time it was filled with afterhour's clubs, gambling, prostitution, and bootlegging. A hang-out for Vancouver's black community, Hogan's Alley was really just a collection of horse stables, small cottages and shacks where the west side crowd came for a walk on the wild side. The alley ran between Union and Prior from Gore to Main Street and was most likely named for Harry Hogan, a black singer who lived in an apartment at **406 Union Street** at the corner of Dunlevy in 1921. The 1915 apartment building, renumbered to 406 Union Street, replaced the house at 806 Dunlevy—one of the identical houses that originally bordered Richardson's house.

Another colourful member of the early black community in Strathcona was Nora Hendrix. Between 1938 and 1952 this grandmother of rocker Jimi Hendrix lived at **827 East Georgia**. Born in Tennessee, Nora (nee Moore) was a dancer in a vaudeville troupe. She met and married Ross Hendrix, a former Chicago policeman and later, in a bizarre career change, a stagehand for the troupe. They settled in Vancouver and had three children. The youngest, James Allen Hendrix, known as Al, moved to Seattle and at twenty-two, met sixteen-year-old Lucille Peters who gave birth to Jimi Hendrix in 1942. According to *Jimi Hendrix, the Man, the Magic, the Truth*, a biography published in 2004, Jimi lived in fourteen different places, including short stints in Vancouver. "I'd always look forward to seeing Gramma Nora, my dad's mother in Vancouver, usually in the summer," he once told author Sharon Lawrence. "I'd pack some stuff in a brown sack, and then she'd buy me new pants and shirts and underwear. I kept getting taller and growing out of all my clothes, and my shoes were always a falling-apart disgrace. Gramma would tell me little Indian stories that had been told to her when she was my age. I couldn't wait to hear a new story. She had Cherokee blood. So did Gramma Jeter. I was proud of that, it was in me too."

Shortly after Hendrix left the army in 1962, he hitchhiked two thousand miles to Vancouver and stayed several weeks with Nora. He picked up some cash sitting in with a group at a club known as Dante's Inferno. Six years later when the Jimi Hendrix Experience played the Pacific Coliseum, one reviewer described the band as "bigger than Elvis." Hendrix, dressed all in white, played hits such as "Fire," "Hey Joe," and "Voodoo Child," and at one point acknowledged his grandmother, who sat in the audience, and launched into "Foxy Lady."

When Carole Itter and Daphne Marlatt interviewed Nora Hendrix in the 1970s for *Opening Doors: Vancouver's East End,* she was in her nineties. "The house was full of music, there was a picture rail where she had all the record covers of Jimi Hendrix and

RECENT SHOT OF 827 GEORGIA
ST. (FORMER HOME OF NORA
HENDRIX, GRANDMOTHER OF
LEGENDARY ROCKER, JIMI
HENDRIX)
PHOTO BY JAMES JOHNSTONE

other family musicians," says Itter. Hendrix entertained them with her stories, her laughter, and her memories of extreme discrimination against black people in Vancouver. "She was a very old, very energetic lady," recalls Itter.

Itter, a visual artist and author, moved to Strathcona in 1974. At that time rents were cheap, houses were large, and Strathcona was a haven for artists. Since 1986 she's lived at **543 Hawks Avenue**, at the corner of Keefer, in a three-storey duplex, part of a complex of buildings called the Kirby Block that contain eleven units and a grocery store. The DeCamillis family, one of Vancouver's early Italian immigrant families, bought the Kirby Block in 1929. It stayed in the family until 2006. In 1977, David DeCamillis, then sixty-four, told Itter that his mother raised four children there in the 1930s. "The average net rent we'd collect from twelve units here would be from two to thirty-nine dollars a month to look after five people. That was the days before supermarkets, so in the store we had all kinds of groceries, two or three employees. Back of the store was a bookie joint for horse races, then in one section of the store, there was a shoemaker's shop, but he went broke, then a butcher came in and he went broke."

A FEISTY NEIGHBOURHOOD

Across the road from the Kirby Block at 803 Keefer on the corner of Hawks, David DeCamillis ran the Western Cartage Gym. The East End put out its share of prize fighters. Angelo Branca, as well as being a barrister and a judge, was also the middleweight champion of Canada in the 1930s. Branca, along with others from the neighbourhood such as Roy Callegeri and Felice DiPalma, trained at DeCamillis' gym. DiPalma (or Phil Palmer as he was later called) was born in Civitanova, Italy in 1922. He lived at **716 Hawks Avenue** from 1929 to 1946 and then at an almost identical house at **712 Hawks**. Raymond Culos says it was a sad story. "They just threw Phil in a bit too early and he was fodder for the people who could make a buck out of him," says Culos. "Poor bugger came back hearing bells ringing in his head." By 1946 he had fought forty-one professional fights at

Madison Square Garden. According to Boxrec Boxing Encyclopaedia, Palmer's record was fifty-two wins (twenty by knock-out), twenty-one losses, and seven draws.

A story in Raymond Culos' book, *Vancouver's Society of Italians,* explains DiPalma's name change to Palmer. Jimmy Ricci tells Culos that as a teenager DiPalma was an altar boy at Sacred Heart Church in Strathcona when he caught a thief stealing a chalice from the unlocked church. "[Phil] saw this guy take off and gave chase. He caught up with him and started to fight with him, pushing, shoving, pummelling all the way down the Keefer Street Hill. Beat the crap out of the guy and returned the chalice to the church. An onlooker said, 'you are good with your fists. Why don't you become a fighter?' The men at the Junior G-Men's Club realized that he had great natural ability and skill, and the trainer asked Phil to let him put his name on that week's fight card. Phil's replied that if his mother ever found out he was boxing, she would kill him. 'Then let's change your name to Phil Palmer,' suggested the trainer."

In 2002 the gym turned into Koo's Auto Service, a garage that is now part of an up market six-townhouse complex.

Jimmy Archibald McLarnin, the 5'6", two-time world welterweight champion, was one of the best known boxers to come out of Vancouver in the 30s. Born in 1906 in Inchicore, Ireland, he arrived in Vancouver at age nine accompanied by his parents and eleven siblings. He began boxing the following year, won his first pro fight at age thirteen and his first World title in 1933. All together, "Baby Face" McLarnin won sixty-two out of seventy-six pro fights and retired at twenty-nine with more than three hundred thousand dollars in the bank.

Sam McLarnin, Jimmy's father, ran a second-hand furniture shop, and in 1920 they lived at **662 Union Street** in a small Queen Anne with gingerbread trim perched high above the street. By the 1930s, McLarnin lived at **1466 William Street** in the Grandview/Woodlands area. The three-storey Victorian house is now painted a bright teal with yellow trim around the windows. McLarnin eventually retired to California. He was inducted into the Boxing Hall of Fame in 1991 and died in 2004, aged 96.

LITERARY LEGENDS

Author Wayson Choy grew up in the East End, and the area is the setting for two of his books—*The Jade Peony,* published in 1995 and his 1999 memoir *Paper Shadows: a Chinatown Childhood.* Choy's mother was a meat cutter and sausage stuffer in a

Chinatown factory, and his father cooked onboard Canadian Pacific Ships. When he was six, the family moved to a simple Edwardian house at **630 Keefer Street.** Behind the once blue paint and peeling white window frames, the two-storey house has a bay window, a stained glass flower motif in the front left hand corner, a front porch, and Doric columns. Today, the house nestles between a Vancouver Special on one side, and what was once the Good Shepherd Mission, now a private house, on the other.

Another well known writer and historian, Paul Yee, lived near the Choy's during the 1970s at **540 Heatley Street** at the corner of Keefer. A simple three-storey stucco house, it sits at street level. Yee, who is a third generation Chinese Canadian, wrote a number of widely read children's books as well as *Saltwater City: The story of Vancouver's Chinese Community.* Before moving to Heatley Street, Yee lived at 350-and-a-half East Pender Street. The house is no longer there, but the half has an interesting history. "The half refers to a smaller house which stood at the rear of the main house behind the fire-wood barn," explains Yee who now lives in Toronto. "Maybe it was meant for servants." The family left the house in 1968 to live above the Yees family store on East Pender. After the Heatley address, following the pattern of many immigrants, the Yees moved east into the Grandview Woodlands neighbourhood.

STRATHCONA ELEMENTARY SCHOOL

Choy, Lee and thousands of other immigrant families attended Strathcona Elementary, one of Vancouver's oldest schools. School enrolment in the 1930s included Japanese, Chinese, Italians, Jews, some Scandinavians, Russians, Ukrainians, and blacks. John Atkin writes in *The Greater Vancouver Book* that the Japanese made up nearly half the student population. "While there were no strict boundaries within the neighbourhood, many of the Japanese lived on the north side of Hastings Street, while the Italian community primarily occupied Union and Prior Streets. Between these two groups were the Ukrainian Hall, built in 1928 at Hawks and Pender, and one block west at Heatley, the Schara Tzedeck Synagogue," writes Atkin. "The 1908 Fountain Chapel on Jackson at Prior (previously the German, then Norwegian, Lutheran Church) was the spiritual home for Vancouver's small black population. The growing Chinese population lived on the edges of Chinatown."

Opposite the school sits **602 Keefer.** Built in 1902, the Principal's house, as it's known, is an impressive mix of late Victorian and Queen Anne, with a witches-hat turret, stained-glass windows, ornate bargeboards, gable roofs, and a magical garden—a legacy from a more recent landscaper-owner. From the tall gunnera with its giant leaves to the red clematis, palms, fig and willow tree, it's a playful garden that, in 2006, beat out sixty-five entries from all over Vancouver to win the Vancouver Park Board sponsored Up Front Garden Contest.

Gregory Henry Tom, the school's first principal, bought the corner lot from the Vancouver Improvement Company for four hundred and twenty dollars and paid another one thousand dollars for a house, designed and built by William Cline. Not a bad deal at a time when the average Strathcona lot was selling for between two-hundred-and-fifty and two-thousand dollars. Apparently Tom, a short guy with dark hair and moustache, who had a reputation for making frequent and enthusiastic use of the strap, built the house so the upstairs window faced the school ground and he could watch the children play outside. The sound of the window opening meant at least one child would be sitting outside the principal's office for the rest of the day, and probably be sore the next. In *The Story of Strathcona School*, a former vice-principal describes Tom as strict and unsympathetic. "A strong disciplinarian, Mr. Tom is remembered by all former students as 'a good teacher, but very strict, not having much sympathy for excuses or human weakness'."

Today's Strathcona is made up of families, artists, retirees, and young single professionals, residing in one of the densest and more liveable areas of the city. In late spring and summer, black-eyed susans, pink cone flowers, and an array of daisies spill out of gardens onto sidewalks, and the tiny parks provide play space for kids and dogs and fill with the various ethnic faces of the city.

Strathcona also has an amazing stretch of nineteenth and twentieth century architecture. Small cottages, brightly coloured Queen Annes with gingerbread trim, Arts and Crafts, and Edwardians painted periwinkle with white trim boards colour the neighbourhood. Tall skinny houses squeeze onto twenty-five foot lots, while others sit high above the street reached by steep stairs and painted in bright blues and reds, pinks, yellows, and greens. Later additions are accessed by lanes that rise and dip with the landscape.

In some ways, the story of Strathcona is one of survival. Its early inhabitants were mostly the British working class immigrants, which over time changed to the Japanese, Jewish, Russian, Italian, and Chinese. These early immigrants worked in sawmills, at the railway, and at the port. They survived the Depression and the two World Wars through hard work and ingenuity. They faced racial discrimination and desperate poverty, and although many could barely speak English, they took on three governments to save Strathcona from "urban renewal" in the 1960s.

And, unlike in the United States where it lasted from 1920 to 1933, Prohibition was short-lived in B.C. By the 1930s Vancouver was deep into the Depression and desperation combined with antiquated liquor laws allowed Vancouver's bootlegging industry to flourish. People like Maria Piovesan and Karolina Fedychyn were small-time bootleggers. The bigger ones stayed in the wholesaling end of the business, delivering to the clubs, and many made a lot of money selling whisky and beer to the speakeasies, unlicensed clubs, and high-profile citizens.

Then there were the liquor barons, the truly rich, who made fortunes from their breweries and staggering profits from shipping liquor to the States during Prohibition. The mansions of the liquor barons were, of course, on the west side of town.

Chapter 2

RUM RUNNERS AND LIQUOR BARONS

While those on the Eastside of town struggled through the 1920s and '30s, avoiding police raids and discrimination, on the other side of Vancouver, liquor barons built Hollywood-style mansions, opened a downtown dance club, and bought up hundreds of hectares of both farm and recreational properties. B.C.'s Prohibition did little to quell profits, and supplying the booze to thirsty Americans during the U.S. Prohibition made brewers head-spinning sums of money.

The Reifel family, probably best known today for the peaceful Reifel Migratory Bird Sanctuary in Ladner, brewed the family fortune. Henry Reifel, a Bavarian born brew master, was a founder of the Canadian Brewing & Malting Company at Yew Street and Eleventh Avenue in 1908 (now owned by Carling O'Keefe). Later, the company became Vancouver Breweries, adding another four breweries and two distilleries to the family holdings. Henry's two sons, George Conrad and Henry (Harry) Frederick, went off to brewing school, first in Nanaimo and then in Vancouver, before joining the family business. In 1917, Prohibition hit British Columbia, and Henry and George sailed off to Japan, building and operating the Anglo-Japanese Brewing Company, the country's first brewery where they developed the technique to produce malt from rice. Once it became established, they sold their interests in the brewery and returned to Vancouver.

Building a fortune based on beer didn't exactly endear the Reifels to Vancouver's early establishment, but it did provide the money for the family to live beside them. In 1925, Henry Reifel moved from a house on West Twelfth Avenue to a much more upmarket Tudor Revival style house at **1451 Angus Drive** in Shaughnessy, near both sons. George and his wife Alma lived at Angus Drive and King Edward next door to Harry and Edna's large Georgian style house. About this time, Harry must have been planning his move to "millionaire's row" on Southwest Marine Drive.

The Kerrisdale enclave housed a who's who of Vancouver. Large acreages and massive houses, hidden down long tree-lined, gated driveways, overlooked the river. The first residents to move to the area around 1910 included John Tucker, president of the Vancouver Lumber Company, his son-in-law Edward Knight, and W.H. Malkin, the wholesale grocer and one-time mayor of Vancouver. In the early 1920s, George Kidd, the general manager of B.C. Electric Railway, William Dick, the Hastings Street clothier, and Gordon Farrell, president of B.C. Telephone Co., also built their houses on Southwest Marine Drive, as did Philip Rogers, son of sugar baron B.T. Rogers. None of the houses of these established gentry were quite as lavish as Harry Reifel's Rio Vista.

RIO VISTA

By 1930, Harry and Edna Reifel had moved into **2170 Southwest Marine Drive**, the Spanish Colonial Revival house, with the name meaning "River View." Bernard Cuddon Palmer, a British born architect and son of a brewer's agent, designed the mansion. His credentials included a stint with the famous Samuel Maclure before striking out on his own.

In 1932, Katherine Rempel was fourteen and living at a rooming house run by the Mennonite Brethren Church at Forty-ninth Avenue and Fraser Street that helped young girls find housekeeping jobs during the Depression. Originally from Orenberg in Russia, she was a German speaking Mennonite who, at the age of seven, had fled religious persecution with her large family sailing first to Montreal, then taking the train to Saskatchewan and finally to a small farm in Abbotsford, B.C.

One morning, Edna Reifel called the home looking for a maid to join her large staff at Rio Vista. The Mennonite home worked on a seniority system and Katherine's roommate was next up for a job. She offered to pay the seven-cent streetcar fare if Katherine would go with her. Katherine clearly remembers the first time she saw Rio Vista. Sitting high on a bluff above the Fraser River next door to the Shaughnessy Golf and Country Club, the house had a tiled roof, cast stone ornamentation, a spectacular conservatory, ten fireplaces, a sunken ballroom, a library with walnut panelling, a billiard room, and a full-size tavern. The property tax assessment records for 1932 show Rio Vista valued at $125,000 and the value of the land at $14,210.

A gardener led the two girls past a tiled Pompeian swimming pool, through lavish gardens and past a four-car garage. "It was beautiful. You came in, and there was this beautiful staircase that went round and round and you'd stand there and look down into this foyer," she says. "There were huge rooms with hand paintings on the walls. There were quarters in the basement for the Chinese cook. The ballroom was in the basement and there was dancing and movies shown."

While Edna Reifel interviewed her friend, Katherine remembers sitting very still. "I'm sitting there looking around not saying anything, and when she was finished, Mrs. Reifel said, 'I'll take you.' That was me." It wasn't altogether surprising. The Reifel's staff was almost entirely German speaking and even though Katherine hadn't spoken during the interview, her heritage was recognizable by her last name.

Katherine quickly fit in with the rhythm of the household, working alongside a cook, two gardeners and a nursemaid for the two little girls, Barbara Ann Mariel and Betty Joan Lorraine. Katherine's room in the third floor servant's quarters was comfortable, and Thursday was her one day off. "I had to wait on the tables and keep the stairways and entrance clear," she says. "I had very little to do, to tell you the truth. It was the best job I ever had."

The Reifels spent many weekends at their farm. Katherine remembers one party that the staff threw in the rarely used ballroom. "We had this big shindig, it was hopping with people. We were drinking their liquor and dancing all night long," she says. "They were only in Langley; it wasn't an hour and a half away. If they'd decided to come home, we would have all been canned."

Katherine was often a recipient of Mrs. Reifel's old clothing. "There was a closet full of fur coats, real fur coats, and shoes like a shoe store, and then there were the hats," she says. "Another closet was full of clothes; but she was generous, and she would give us stuff and it would last forever. We did learn good taste."

Katherine describes the Reifels as down to earth. Edna Reifel's father was a streetcar driver and, she says, Edna's parents always looked out of place when they visited. "She obviously wasn't born into society, so society didn't accept her. So all that money didn't do them much good," says Katherine. About two years later, when Katherine left to get married, Edna Reifel presented her with a silver cream and sugar bowl set.

Following Harry Reifel's death in 1973, Rio Vista sold to Vancouver philanthropist and self-made businessman, Joe Segal.

BELLA VISTA

At the same time Segal bought Rio Vista for $500,000, he also bought Harry Reifel's property at **6270 Glover Road, Milner** near Langley for $800,000. The farm sits on rolling green fields with views of Mount Baker and Golden Ears. John Jolly bought the hundred acre land parcel for $2,700 in 1883. He sold the property to a Dr. Wessell who built the house in 1920 as a weekend retreat. Reifel bought the farm in 1930—evidently a booming year for the brewing industry—and bred jersey cows, ran a dairy and built a three-quarter mile training track for race horses.

The farm house is a story-book cottage, like one you'd expect to see in the English countryside, with window seats, nooks, elaborate wood mouldings, and a tall curving ceiling in the living room. It sits behind a large fence and cedar hedge on a busy stretch of highway, and its steeply pitched shingled roof is clearly visible from the street. The original barn burned down in 1947, and Reifel built an attractive white gambrel roofed structure with a green roof and window trim that was later turned into residences. Segal says he was no farmer, but he'd fallen in love with the magnificent craftsmanship and superb quality of Rio Vista on Southwest Marine Drive. When he put in an offer for Rio Vista he found that a foreign buyer was set to close the deal, not only to buy Rio Vista, but also to purchase the Reifel's Langley property. "I bought the farm to get the house," says Segal. "The woodwork and the finishings were unbelievable—there was nothing of that quality ever built in the city," he says of Rio Vista.

His wife Rosalie, says Segal, had other ideas. "I came home and said to my wife I bought her [Rio Vista]. I took her out there and there was a wonderful bridge on the property between the house and the coach house and I said to my wife, I've bought the house and I've bought the farm, and she said, 'You gave me everything I didn't want.'"

Segal says he spent another one million dollars and two years restoring Rio Vista. As for the farm, he says, he hung onto it and farmed it for another five money-losing years before selling it to a group of investors. According to an article in the *Langley Times* in 1994, the investors were a group of Langley doctors who lost money on the property and flipped it to the owners of the Cloverdale Raceway and Orangeville Raceways who rented it out to a series of tenants over the years until selling to Greg Ardron in 1997.

THE REIFEL HUNTING LODGE

While Harry was building Rio Vista in the late 1920s, George Reifel commissioned Vancouver architect Ross Lort to design a hunting lodge at his property on Westham Island just outside Ladner. An outdoorsman who liked to hunt and fish, Reifel had brought associates to the area to hunt ducks and geese since the early 1920s. He bought the land and tidal flats on the south arm of the Fraser River in 1927 and went about creating a complex of dikes, three freshwater sloughs, and large feed areas for the birds. Even in those days it would have been hugely expensive. Piles driven into the Fraser River held the sand, which was hydraulically pumped and dredged and dams were installed where the river split into three narrow channels. In an interview recorded in 1981 with Rita Fradley and Gay Trevitt, George Reifel's son, also named George, says his father was able to reclaim about one hundred acres. George junior, who was seven in 1929, says that by the end of that year his father had dyked and dammed the whole property at the same time that he was building the lodge. "All the material was brought in by boat, by barge, the lumber, the workmen, everything, because there were no roads extending from Westham Island to the place—it was an isolated package," he says.

Now the offices for the Canadian Wildlife Service, the old hunting lodge at **5421 Robertson Road** is a huge rambling two-storey wooden framed house on a plantation-style lawn and reached by a drive lined with pruned cedars. Set close to the water it has the original lookout tower, and old dugouts (holes dug into the ground where hunters lie in wait for prey) can still be seen in the slough. Inside, the beams and plank floor are still intact, and the garage has the original wood doors and multi-paned windows.

When the Reifels occupied the house, what is now office space was a guest wing with seven bedrooms and a games room. The original river rock chimney still stands painted white with an engraving of a large hunting dog over the fireplace. At one time, the room held a large collection of stuffed game birds, a huge mounted elk's head and a selection of hunting trophies, hand carved decoys, and rows of expensive shotguns. In its heyday as a hunting lodge, the grounds had barns, dog kennels, gardens, a swimming pool, and tennis court.

Mostly ducks and geese flocked to Reifel Island to feast on the grain brought in from the family's New Westminster distillery. George Reifel junior told the interviewer that they fed the birds between eight hundred and one thousand pounds of grain a day, and in those days, hunters were allowed to shoot twenty-five ducks a day. "My father enjoyed the hunting, but he was not a game hog," says the younger Reifel. "But I wouldn't call him a conservationist either. He knew whatever birds escaped B.C. would probably be shot in Washington, Oregon, California, or Mexico, so he might as well invite some of his friends."

Reifel says by 1933 the river's virgin alluvial silt produced golden rod, willows, thistles—"everything imaginable." They cleared another three-hundred odd acres on Westham Island, and after the summer house burned down in Crescent Beach, began to spend more time on the farm. In those days Westham Island was reachable only by ferry from Ladner.

Young George Reifel graduated from UBC in 1944 with a degree in agriculture. During the Second World War, the Reifel farm produced one-third of all the sugar beet in Canada. Gradually, the younger Reifel moved into farming, growing oats, barley, and grain, and eventually raising cattle and sheep. The Reifels bought up two neighbouring farms, bringing the land to 850 acres. George Reifel grew crops such as green beans and green peas for freezing and canning, cabbages and carrots for their seeds, and barley grain for his cattle.

In 1949, young George Reifel became chairman of Alberta Distillers and moved to Calgary, keeping the farm as a sideline. By the time he inherited the farm in 1958 on the death of his father, he says it had lost its charm. "We got into the farm business by neces-

REIFEL'S HUNTING LODGE, DELTA
USED WITH PERMISSION OF THE DELTA MUSEUM AND ARCHIVES, PHOTO #1989-34-100

sity," he told Fradley and Trevitt in the 1981 interview. "It did not make money, there is no way you are going to get fat on the farm."

In 1963 George Reifel joined forces with Barry Leach, a college professor, and Fred Auger, publisher of *The Province*, to create a waterfowl sanctuary. Reifel leased ninety-eight acres of his land for one dollar a year with the option to purchase, while people like H.R. MacMillan, Clarence Wallace, and Gordon Farrell kicked in sizable donations. In 1972 Reifel sold the waterfowl refuge to the Canadian Wildlife Service for $2.3 million for the land and various buildings. The parcel included the ninety-eight acres already under lease, now gifted to the wildlife services, making the total holdings around fourteen hundred acres, on condition that it remain a sanctuary and that the property keep the family name.

In 1966, George Reifel junior, his wife Norma, three sons and a daughter bought the Green farm at **5992 River Road,** an old white farmhouse with a blue roof and yellow trim around the window frames and a huge front verandah that now stands between large housing developments near the town of Ladner.

CASA MIA

The senior George Reifel must have been happy with his hunting lodge because he commissioned Ross Lort to design a flamboyant Spanish-style colonial villa on five and a half acres of land at **1920 Southwest Marine Drive**, a short distance from Rio Vista. The brightly painted yellow mansion he called Casa Mia is clearly visible from both Southwest Marine and from the banks of the Fraser River.

On a visit to the Vancouver City Archives in 1938, George Reifel told Major James Matthews, the City of Vancouver's first archivist, that, "When I was erecting my house, we dug out the stump of a big tree and beneath it found the remains of an Indian midden. We did not excavate it and it is there yet."

The quiet and reserved Lort lived in the West End of Vancouver with his wife and five children. Bill Lort says his father disliked contracts. He always said, "If you can't look a man in the eye and shake his hand, what good is a piece of paper with two signatures on it?" Even in tough times, Ross Lort would never have asked George Reifel for money. One Saturday morning in 1931 when Lort was at Casa Mia inspecting the Southwest Marine Drive property, likely dressed in his habitual grey flannels and Harris Tweed jacket, Reifel pulled up in his large black car. Dressed in a full-length black coat with a high collar and fedora and puffing on a cigar, he totally terrified the architect. "Lort," boomed Reifel, "I guess you'd like some money wouldn't you?" Not waiting for an answer, Reifel reached into his pocket, pulled out a wad of bills, peeled off a thousand dollar note and handed it to the stunned architect. Only four years old at the time and the youngest of Lort's children, Bill Lort remembers the story as folklore. "My father came home, showed the thousand dollar bill to my mother who damn near died of heart failure looking at it—a family of seven in 1931," he says. Lort and his wife climbed the stairs to the bedroom, pushed back their double bed, rolled up the carpet, put down the thousand dollar bill, rolled back the carpet, then the bed, and took turns sitting on the bed until the bank opened on Monday morning. "My father gave the bill to the manager and the manager had never seen a thousand dollar bill, and he showed it to all the staff in the bank—they had never seen a thousand dollar bill. It was considered very much Chicago, Al Capone, Mafia kind of currency."

Finished by 1932, the four-level house has nine fireplaces, ten bathrooms, a sauna, a ballroom, a four-car garage, and stunning gardens. The master bedroom had a vaulted ceiling, and the floor was decorated by silk carpets. A gown room with cedar-lined closets and an ensuite bathroom with marble trim made the space truly opulent. One story has it that in the middle of rampant unemployment and widespread poverty, George brought up artists from the Walt Disney Studios to hand-paint murals for the third-floor playroom.

Bill Lort remembers one of the quirks of the design of Casa Mia was that George Reifel insisted that there be only a master bedroom and three bedrooms with ensuites for his children Audrey May, George Henry, and Jane. There were eight servant quarters, including the two "Chinamen's rooms," rooms for an upstairs maid, a downstairs maid, a nanny, a cook, and two gardeners. There were no guest rooms. "George Reifel didn't want anyone who wasn't a member of his family sleeping in his house overnight. He told my father that he would pay the Georgia Hotel bill and out of town guests could stay there. He said, 'I won't have anyone who is not family sleeping under my roof'," says Bill Lort. "Audrey, the older daughter, had this huge bedroom, and off the corner of the bedroom is a circular tower, and that was her bathroom, with a bath elevated up steps, a separate shower stall, basin, and toilet. You could hold a cocktail party in the bathroom."

Casa Mia's full-size art-deco ballroom also had one of a handful of sprung floors in the city, another being at the Reifel-owned Commodore Ballroom. Rubber tires and horsehair inserted under the dance floor created a spring so that when lots of people stepped onto it, it felt like jumping on a trampoline. And, Depression it might have been, but on December 3, 1930 the Commodore Ballroom on Granville Street, a two-storey building with a semi-circular bandstand, opened to a sold-out crowd of fifteen hundred.

One popular dance band that made regular appearances at the Commodore in the late 1930s was Charlie Pawlett and the Commodores. Pawlett played trumpet, banjo, and violin and even rated an entry in the 1937 *Who's Who in Western Canada*. In 1940, Pawlett and his family lived at **2645 West Fifth Avenue,** a three-storey Kitsilano kit house ordered from a catalogue. It sat on a narrow lot and looked much like every other house on the block. In 1946 he bought a house in North Vancouver's Lynn Valley, played at the Second Narrows Supper Club, and was a regular fixture riding his bike down Mountain Highway with his trumpet strapped to the back of the bike. In later years, George Reifel junior, a mad jazz follower, would invite jazz artists such as Dizzie Gillespie, Stan Kenton, and Count Basie back to Casa Mia for late night parties and jam sessions.

ROSS LORT

While the Reifels entertained lavishly at Casa Mia, Ross Lort was building his own reputation. Early in his career he had worked with renowned architect Samuel Maclure and in the 1920s designed the English Arts and Crafts-style houses at 3057 and 3075 West Thirty-ninth Avenue, the Park Lane Apartments at 975 Chilco and the Queen Anne Garden Apartments at 1235 Nelson Street. In 1937 he showed his versatility with a striking modern two-storey concrete cube house at 3846 West Tenth Avenue designed for Horace G. Barber, a civil engineer. It was the first known use of exposed concrete for a residence in Vancouver. Lort designed a Spanish Colonial Revival-style beauty school for Madame Maxine at 1215 Bidwell Street and was the architect for the Western Society Physical Rehabilitation Centre (now G.F. Strong) at 4255 Laurel Street. Earlier that decade Lort moved his own family to a very conservative heritage house at **2080 West Thirty-fifth Avenue** in Shaughnessy, behind a stone fence and with what real estate agents would call a mature garden. It couldn't be further away from the flamboyant Casa Mia on Southwest Marine Drive or the edgy Barber residence on West Tenth Avenue.

In 1950, Lort won the commission to design the extension to the Vancouver Art Gallery to house a donation of work by the late Emily Carr. The Art Gallery needed some land on Georgia Street which, at the time, had a row of single family homes sitting on thirty-three-foot lots owned by the Reifels.

As the architect for the Vancouver Art Gallery, Lort asked the Reifels to donate the property. "My father was a very timid, shy man, and he went and spoke to George Reifel who he knew better than Harry, and he was put through this great rigmarole. 'Oh we are accepted now that the other Southwest Marine Drive families want us to donate property,' says Bill Lort. My father said he was terrified. The Reifels were saying finally we are accepted because we've made money and we own property and the culture vultures of the art gallery want us to donate...Of course the Reifel brothers knew from the very start that they were going to donate the property on Georgia Street, but it was quite a struggle for my father because he would never have begged anybody to do a thing like that."

George Reifel died in 1958, and the family sold Casa Mia a decade later to Ross Maclean, a high profile psychiatrist and hospital owner. Maclean had four children, and a host of Hollywood stars who stayed at his hospital also visited the mansion. He later sold the house to Nelson Skalbania in 1980. In the mansion's multiple garages, Skalbania parked his Rolls Royces, his Mercedes-Benz 450 SLs and his prized 1928 Phaeton convertible, which was used in the motion picture "The Great Gatsby." A real-estate developer who attracted media attention in the late 70s by flipping property worth millions of dollars, Skalbania at one time owned a $2.7 million de Havilland jet, a fifty-three metre diesel yacht called Chimon, and sports interests, which included the National Hockey League's Atlanta Flames, the Montreal Alouettes, the Vancouver Canadians, and the Edmonton Oilers.

Shortly after Skalbania's spectacular bankruptcy at the end of 1982, Casa Mia sold to Bruce Branch and his wife Michiyo, the daughter of a Japanese millionaire. Branch hired Ross Lort's son Bill, also an architect, and added another $4.5 million in renovations. In 1998 Casa Mia hit the market with a twenty million dollar price tag, only to be relisted several months later at just under ten million—the result of a mortgage foreclosure action. According to an article in *The Vancouver Sun*, the house, which now sat on a 1.5-acre lot with two hundred and twenty nine feet of frontage, had property taxes set at $26,172 and an assessed value of $4.4 million. The house sold to a numbered company for the fireside price of $4.2 million and, not surprisingly, went up for sale again in May 2000 with a listing price of $6.5 million.

RUM RUNNERS

Possibly it was the size of Rio Vista and Casa Mia, their location near the Fraser River, or just the mystery surrounding rum running in the 1920s and 30s, but for years there were rumours of tunnels that connected the two houses and also led down to the river. Bill Lort, who still has the original house plans, says there were no tunnels in the drawings or any found in the later excavation of the land below the bluff. The tunnels, while a great story, also make little sense. While the act of running booze down to the States broke U.S. laws if caught within the twelve mile limit, there was no Prohibition here at the time, and exporting alcohol was quite legal in Canada as long as all the proper taxes were paid, and for the participants, it was a highly paid adventure.

One of the key players in the rum-running business was Archie McGillis. In the mid-1920s he lived not far from the Reifels at **1747 West Thirty-seventh Avenue** near Marguerite Street in a fairly modest craftsman-style house, painted blue with white trim. In those years the directory listed him as a broker, president of something called the Vancouver-Courtenay and manager of the Giant Salvage Company. McGillis both owned, at least on paper, and captained some of the famed rum-running ships of the time. He was the first captain of the Malahat when it started its illustrious nine-year rum-running career. He initially ran a small office at the foot of Bidwell Street and later moved into a large warehouse on Hamilton Street. During the Prohibition years, McGillis was the owner of record of the Chakawana, bought from the RCMP in the early 1920s and seized in Mexico during the early years of Prohibition while operating out of Ensenada, Mexico. Under the company name Canadian Mexican Shipping Co., he owned the Coal Harbour, a three-masted schooner seized in 1925, the

Ironbark, a motor boat, and the Malahat, a wooden five-masted schooner built in Victoria in 1917 as a lumber carrier. The Malahat became Queen of Rum Row, a floating warehouse that often carried sixty thousand cases of liquor.

Stuart Stone captained the Malahat through most of its rum-running career. His house on Yew Street is no longer there, but his son Jim Stone remembers a community of captains and crew members from the rum-running ships that lived nearby. In the 1930s, Captains Joe Keegan and Charles Hudson lived at a two-storey brick apartment building at **1615 Trafalgar Street** on the corner of Yew Street in Kitsilano, which would give the two sea captains commanding views of English Bay.

Keegan captained the Jessie, a two-masted schooner. In 1928, the Jessie sank in a collision with an unknown vessel one hundred miles west of San Diego. The following year, Captain Keegan was on the seventy-six foot schooner, the Noble, when it wrecked and burned on Escalante Reef, Vancouver Island. Four people died.

The Americans captured the "Coal Harbour" in the 1920s. "We operated perfectly legally," Hudson, the Coal Harbour's captain, told Ruth Greene, author of *Personality Ships of B.C.* "We considered ourselves public philanthropists. We supplied good liquor to poor thirsty Americans who were poisoning themselves with rotten moonshine...We brought prosperity back to the Harbour of Vancouver." Hudson was most famous for devising a system of coded radio communications for two-way communication between the mother ships and shore boats waiting for information on coast guard positions and pick-up ships.

Between 1926 and 1934 Hudson lived at **2828 Waterloo Street** in Kitsilano, but by 1929 he had another house on the hill high above Jericho Beach. Jim Stone's aunt Hazel, who lived with them, used to travel to work as a radio operator for Hudson, taking the street-car up Fourth Avenue and walking the few blocks to reach Hudson's place. "She talked about going on the streetcar and coming back late at night and how she met some people that were almost always on that streetcar, and they were quite curious about her. She had to pretend she was a nurse. Later on, she had to pretend she was a nurse taking care of a pregnant woman, all that kind of thing," says Jim Stone. "She was a very outgoing sort of person, very gregarious. She looked upon it as an adventure."

Stone, who was born in 1919, was mostly proud of his often absent father. "I was quite excited about his adventures," he says. "But around 1926 the attitude towards rum-runners changed somewhat, people tended to look down on them and accept the idea that they were criminals as the Americans had said they were, so it was a mixed feeling that I had, but for the most part I was proud of him."

It was all over by the end of 1933 when the Americans put a stop to Prohibition. The following July, *The Vancouver Sun* ran a story tucked away in the business section with the curious head-line: "Reifels have resigned." Not much longer than a brief, the story reprinted part of a statement from the board of directors of Brewers and Distillers of Vancouver Ltd., the "best known liquor company of the Pacific Coast." The board, it transpires, had accepted the resignation of Henry Reifel and his two sons Harry and George because of "allegations" that some of their products had found their way down into the United States during U.S. Prohibition.

Six days later *The Province* ran a slightly larger story, "Reifels are indicted," with a subhead, "Seattle Grand Jury charges Vancouver brewers with conspiracy." What was even more interesting than burying the story between a picture of "hunger marchers" in Queen's Park, Toronto and an ad for self-supporting elastic-top hose, was that you had to read half-way down the story to find out that Seattle's Attorney-General was going after the Reifel family in a civil suit for a staggering $17,250,000.

"The indictments charge the pair with landing liquor in Seattle without reporting to customs and without a permit to import dutiable merchandise. The secret landings, the governor declared, were at Seola Beach, a secluded shore land at the Salmon River out-let in Oregon." The Reifels, according to the indictment, were accused of bringing 2,288 cases of assorted liquors, twenty kegs of malt, twelve five gallon jugs of rum and seventy-four bottles of miscellaneous intoxicants. "The alleged operations included the formation of special companies and the use of a fleet of boats, some of which were direct-ed by radio from British Columbia." The case eventually settled out of court for $700,000.

Chapter 3

LAW AND DISORDER

Len Cuthbert, thirty-four, sat in a locked police car in a lane near Heatley Avenue surrounded by a dozen large and angry men. Bricks smashed the car windows and a large axe shattered the cruiser's headlights. Several men half lifted, half dragged Cuthbert out of the broken car, pounded his ribs, and slammed his head with a boulder. He was alive, but unconscious, his face a bloody mess. Fellow officers took him to General Hospital where he eventually recovered from a fractured skull.

Cuthbert was one of more than sixty people hurt in the June 1935 battle of Ballantyne Pier, as a thousand longshoremen, and a smattering of wives and sympathizers marched in columns of four down Heatley Avenue towards the pier determined to get to the ships after a two-week-imposed lockout and strike. When the marchers refused to turn back, police shot a tear gas canister into the crowd setting off a full-scale riot. Twice during the afternoon, police raided and threw tear gas into the longshoreman's headquarters on East Hastings Street. Mayor Gerry McGeer blamed communist agitators for inciting the riot and called it an "open declaration of war, unparalleled in the history of Vancouver."

The '30s were tough years in Vancouver. Men roamed the streets panhandling, begging, and knocking on doors looking for food or handouts. One shantytown under the Georgia Viaduct had at least two hundred and fifty men living among rotting garbage and open toilets. By 1935, there were over two hundred relief camps set up in the province to house men who laboured on public works for twenty cents a day plus food and shelter. The cost of relief in Vancouver soared to $2.7 million a year.

BERNIE "WHISTLING" SMITH

Bernie Smith was twelve years old in 1935. By the age of fourteen he was working for Joe Philliponi, an Italian who had arrived in Vancouver in the early 1930s. Philliponi owned and ran Eagle-Time Delivery Systems, a bike courier system. Philliponi called Smith "Speed Ball 21." When Philliponi asked him what he wanted to do with his life, Smith told him he wanted to be a policeman. "He actually encouraged me," says Smith. Smith signed up with the army at seventeen and five years later joined the Vancouver Police Department—the same year that Philliponi opened the Penthouse Cabaret on Seymour Street. A well-known supper club, its headliners included Sammy Davis Junior and George Burns. The vice squad closed the club in 1975 and charged Philliponi with living off the avails of prostitution. After Philliponi's 1983 murder, Smith, along with a crowd of several hundred, including judges, businessmen and dancers, attended his funeral at Christ Church Cathedral on Burrard Street.

Although a couple of decades younger than Len Cuthbert, Smith would eventually get to know the older man. But where Smith was to start his career associating with criminals, it was Cuthbert who ended up in their pocket.

Unlicensed supper clubs and cabarets, and the absence of all-night liquor stores allowed an already established bootlegging culture to thrive in Vancouver. Raids on private homes and clubs became a regular occurrence, but did little to stop the drinking. Customers of the clubs paid exorbitant cover charges and, once in, wildly inflated prices for mixers and ice. Bottles of rum or whisky that customers brought into the club concealed in paper bags were surreptitiously stashed under the table during the frequent police raids, the customers adamantly denying any knowledge of them.

As a detective in the liquor squad, Smith, who earned his nickname for whistling while he patrolled the streets, spent many nights in and outside of the clubs. "It was part of a way of life, and as a policeman, I didn't feel like crawling on my hands and knees under a table looking for a bottle of whisky, so we would try and get them before they went in," he says. The police took the confiscated liquor to the station, and would later return it for a fifteen-dollar "service charge."

WALLY "BLONDIE" WALLACE

By June 1955 the Vancouver City Police liquor detail had listed eighty-seven bootlegging joints in Vancouver, nearly half of them in constant operation. A written report to the police commission added that there were twenty-seven known "drink-in" establishments and at least sixteen known bottle delivery sources.

While Smith busted every bootlegger he caught it was an uneasy relationship. Like others on the force, he'd grown up on the Eastside. "You must understand," he says. "Bootlegging was a violation of the Provincial Government Liquor Act, it wasn't a criminal offence. The government could have stopped it by opening a liquor store any time at all. They were making money both ways: the money from the bootleggers when they bought from the government, and the fines that they got when they caught them. They sold them the stuff then fined them for selling it."

Smith says he knew Wally "Blondie" Wallace, one of the larger bootleggers of the Strathcona area, very well. Wallace purchased the Piovesan's house at **446 Union Street** in the early 1940s and operated a thriving business from the garage just off a lane at the back of the house. "In those days you'd phone the number and send somebody out to do deliveries and Blondie Wallace had a good business," says Smith. "We'd stake the place out and grab the cars as they came out. He'd have four or five drivers, and they'd be at all different places and they'd have cheap cars in case they got caught." Wallace was a neighbourhood hero, dodging the cops in his bootlegging operation by night and teaching the local kids to box in the basement of his house during the day.

The first time a bootlegger was caught, they were fined; the second time they went to jail. Caught with liquor in the car, both the liquor and the car became the property of the crown. "In about 1950, Blondie Wallace had a brand new Chrysler and he got arrested for bootlegging from the car. The car was seized and he gets three months in Oakalla," says Smith. "Hugh Christie was the warden and when they seized the car, they gave the warden the car and there's Blondie Wallace watching the warden drive his car."

JOHN CAMERON

The relationship between the law breakers and the law enforcers was a fascinating one. The king of the bawdyhouses and a major bootlegger was an Italian named Joe Celona who, at least in the early '30s, was quite friendly with chief of police John Cameron. Cameron, who lived in a narrow three-storey weatherboard house at **2825 Ontario Street** in Mount Pleasant, just off Twelfth Avenue, had a short and disastrous reign. An investigation found that the two had cruised around Howe Sound in a police boat sipping cocktails and entertained by a piper from the police pipe band. Later, when Celona and Chief Cameron were charged with conspiring to affect a public mischief, Celona admitted that he had been on board the police boat, but that he was helping the police track down American gangsters who were planning to rob a B.C. Electric armoured truck from their Bowen Island hide out. Cameron beat a charge of conspiracy to corrupt administration of the force, but in 1935 Mayor Gerry McGeer fired Cameron and seventeen officers. Ironically, after a lengthy fight in the courtroom and through the media, Angelo Branca, the East End lawyer, eventually had the seventeen officers reinstated.

Elected on a mandate to fight crime, McGeer vowed that he would get rid of slot machines and do away with all gambling, book-making, white slavery, and corruption in the police force. In a 1934 campaign speech, his face red and big hands flying, he roared at the audience, "I'm going to clean up on the criminals. Look at them—friends of the mayor [L.D. Taylor]—friends of the Chief of Police; why, Chief Cameron even takes that notoriously evil white-slaver Joe Celona out for cruises in the police boat! And the gamblers, they're operating wide open. You can see for yourself that they must be paying lots of money to policemen to look the other way. Well you can tell those thugs that Gerry is coming, and if they know what's good for them, they will get out of town."

LOUIS DENISON TAYLOR

Known as L.D., Taylor was the most oft elected mayor in the city of Vancouver. He won nine elections, lost seven, and served eight terms between 1910 and 1934

L.D. published and edited the *B.C. Mining Record*, the *Oil and Mining Record* and the *Critic*, a paper on public issues. While a photo of L.D. shows him as a slight looking, bland little man in owlish glasses, he was actually a flamboyant risk taker known for his trademark red tie and cigar. In 1905, Taylor bought the *Vancouver World* newspaper from Sara McLagan, the sister of noted architect Samuel Maclure, and rode the real estate boom so that *The World*, one of four daily newspapers in Vancouver, carried the most display advertising of any daily in North America. In keeping with his mega ambitions, L.D. built a Beaux-Arts seventeen-storey landmark building at 100 West Pender Street to house his newspaper. It was the highest building in the British Empire at the time, beating out Alvo von Alvensleben's Dominion Tower. The building caused a minor scandal at the time for its nine near-naked women sculpted by Charles Marega to support a cornice halfway up the building. The owners of *The Vancouver Sun* bought the building in 1937, and gave it its current name, the Sun Tower.

According to a biography by Daniel Francis, L.D. was an American, born in Ann Arbor, Michigan, with a bit of a shady past. Francis writes that Taylor left Chicago—possibly to avoid being caught for taking deposits from customers when he knew that the bank he had an interest in was insolvent. He was also briefly married to two women at the same time, so Canada must have seemed like a very good idea.

Despite his shaky start, L.D. was a popular mayor during his many terms. He supported the progressive idea of an eight-hour work day, universal suffrage for women, property taxation based on land, city planning, and regional cooperation.

The City built Taylor Manor at **851 Boundary Road** in 1915 as a dormitory for destitute seniors. The old house had separate entrances for men and women. Although Taylor still lends his name to the huge Tudor house, he never lived there. The house was originally called the Vancouver Old People's Home. In 1946, the City renamed the house Taylor Manor, and in the 1960s, after L.D. died, it became a fifty-eight-bed licensed care facility for seniors. In 1917, L.D. lived on the top floor of a seven-storey brick apartment building called Caroline Court at **1058 Nelson Street** on the corner of Thurlow in Vancouver's West End. Built in 1912, it would have been quite majestic in its day, with its green awnings and window trim and two stone lions placed on either side of the front entrance. By 1920, L.D. lived under meagre circumstances at the Granville Mansions at Robson and Granville until his death in 1946. The building lasted until the '60s when it was demolished to make way for the Eaton Centre.

L.D. had a relaxed approach to gambling, bootlegging, and prostitution. In a *Province* article in 1924, he told a reporter he didn't believe that it was the mayor's job to make Vancouver a "Sunday school town," likely fighting words for Gerry McGeer.

GERRY MCGEER

In his first week as mayor, McGeer confiscated one thousand slot machines, and he and his family spent most of 1935 under heavy police guard. A lawyer, and later MP, MLA, and Senator, McGeer married Charl Spencer in 1917, daughter of Victoria's David Spencer, the department store owner. Charl brought a dowry of one hundred dollars a month to the marriage, which later increased to two hundred dollars after the death of her father. McGeer was pulling in around fifteen thousand dollars a year through his law practice and the couple and their cook/housekeeper were able to move into a blue Craftsman style house built around 1920 on a tree-lined street at **4522 West Third**

Avenue in West Point Grey. McGeer, a notorious drinker, would retrieve his nightly bottle of whiskey from its hiding place in the garden, sit back in his corner study by the orange Art Deco fireplace and, if he chose, take in the sunset over English Bay and the North Shore mountains.

By 1925, McGeer was well established and able to buy a larger, more opulent gated house a few blocks away at **4812 Belmont Avenue** for $25,000, as well as a Stutz Bear-cat, a sleek, black four-door car with windows made of shatterproof glass to park in the new garage. It was a huge house with a big garden and a killer view, just from a slightly different angle then his former residence. Belmont Avenue is also the same street that today houses Joe Segal, the former owner of Harry Reifel's Rio Vista, Peter Brown, founder of Canaccord Capital, and Hassan Khosrowshahi, founder of Future Shop.

As mayor of Vancouver during 1935 and 1936, McGeer pushed for the new site of City Hall at its current Mount Pleasant location. In a pitch to investors in June 1935, McGeer told *The Vancouver Sun,* "Work and wages mean better times and prosperity, and is the correct answer to Communism. In raising $1,500,000 for a City Hall, sewers, parks, and lanes, we are providing work and wages, putting money into circulation to help YOUR business and to improve YOUR city. I feel that you owe it to your city and your fellow citizens to help me to expedite the return of confidence and with that PROSPERITY. Your application for BABY BONDS can be made at the Treasurer's office, City Hall."

Although McGeer took credit for selecting the location, at that time considered a long way from the downtown core, former mayor Truman Smith Baxter also claimed the West Twelfth Avenue and Cambie Street address as his idea. The former furniture store owner lived directly across the road from the City Hall site in a large Craftsman-style house built in 1913 at **2740 Yukon Street**. It has wood shingles, stone porch columns, and a distinctive clinker brick cladding. Oddly, the front door and main rooms of the house look not to the spectacular mountain view to the north, but right out onto City Hall.

McGeer forayed into federal politics for a time, but in 1946, he once again ran for mayor. He found the police force still facing corruption charges and a number of well-established bootlegging operations known as blind pigs. In 1943, a man was shot and killed during a holdup attempt at a blind pig on Howe Street. Detective Walter Mulligan solved the case, made superintendent by jumping three ranks and upsetting other more senior officers. In the fall of 1946, when McGeer called for yet another probe into the operation of the force, he fired the current chief for lack of control over his men and appointed Mulligan chief of police, making him the youngest man ever to get the top job.

Mulligan was also the last major appointment McGeer would make before his fatal heart attack in August 1947. In David Williams' 1986 biography *Mayor Gerry*, McGeer's daughter Pat recalls that her fifty-nine-year-old father had come into her bedroom at the Belmont Avenue house to say good night and talk about his recent trip. He reached for a large bottle of eau-de-cologne on her dresser and downed it in one swig. The next morning McGeer's chauffeur found him dressed in pyjamas lying dead on the couch in his study.

WALTER MULLIGAN AND THE VANCOUVER POLICE DEPARTMENT

At forty-two, Mulligan, although relatively young, had a commanding presence. Six foot two and a beefy two hundred and thirty pounds, he was tough, seasoned, confident, and always impeccably dressed. He and his wife Violet lived in a plain white and brown stucco house with a peaked roof and a basement at **1166 East Sixteenth Avenue** in Vancouver. The couple never had children, and Mulligan spent his spare time cultivating prize-winning flowers.

By 1955, Mulligan had seven hundred people under his command. He'd also made a number of enemies. People were talking once again about police corruption and had started pointing fingers at the top cop. The two dailies were aware of stories about the chief's under-the-table bribes, but reluctant to publish anything about it. It wasn't until Len Cuthbert, then a detective sergeant, told his fishing buddy *Province* reporter Eddie Moyer that he was collecting payoffs, that things started to fall apart. *The Province* refused to run the story, so Moyer gave it to Ray Munro, a reporter who quit the paper and took his stories with him. Munro found a kindred spirit in Lou Ruby, publisher of *Flash*, a weekly Toronto scandal paper, and opened a Vancouver office.

Munro, a former spitfire pilot in World War Two, was a colourful character, good looking with a dynamic personality. He carried a forty-five automatic and drove a car equipped with red flashing lights and a siren. As a reporter and photographer, he had a reputation for prancing around the newsroom with a huge pair of shears and cutting off reporter's ties all the while giggling insanely. On June 15, 1955 Munro's story hit the street with a headline that screamed: "Rape of Vancouver! Munro tears mask from crooked law in gangland Eden." The text followed: "A police chief who took a piggy bank—a deputy chief whose secret activities and fits of rage are the talk of a neighbourhood—crooked detectives and enough intrigue to make the fictitious Mike Hammer look like a Lavender Lad—that's the talk of this port city today!" Expecting heavy sales, *Flash* had printed ten thousand extra copies.

Munro lived at **550 Sutherland Avenue** in North Vancouver. According to Jack Webster's autobiography, *Webster!*, Munro drove to Len Cuthbert's house at **186 West Twenty-third Avenue**, a modest grey stucco house on a middle-class street. He went to the door and handed Cuthbert his gun, telling him, "Either you confess and tell the truth or you take this and blow your head off." The next day, Cuthbert tried to do just that. He went to work, sat down at his desk in the police station and tried to shoot himself through the heart with his service revolver. The bullet, which went completely through him, missed his heart by an eighth of an inch. Cuthbert's attempted suicide made the front page of the three Vancouver dailies and sparked the Tupper Royal Commission. Cuthbert was forced to admit to accepting bribes and to testify against his boss, Mulligan.

Cuthbert had a seedy history with the force. Disciplined and demoted for hanging out with criminals and supplying bootlegged liquor to colleagues, in 1945, the police force suspended him for trying to seduce a woman involved in a case he was investigating. Mulligan, according to Cuthbert's testimony, had given him commendations over the years to help him climb back up in rank.

Cuthbert said that both he and Mulligan were doubling their salaries, helped along by Joe Celona who was reportedly paying two hundred dollars a month in bribes. Mulligan never did give evidence. He sat through months of testimony and finally left for the United States where he worked at a California nursery and later as a limo/bus dispatcher before returning to Oak Bay in Victoria to retire. He died there in 1987 at age eighty-three.

At the last day of the inquiry in January 1956, Tupper found that, with the exception of Cuthbert and Mulligan, he couldn't be sure of anyone else's guilt. The Attorney General's office ruled that it didn't have enough evidence to support Tupper's finding of corruption and could not take the case to court.

If Mulligan was taking bribes in a significant way, it didn't show in his possessions. Just after becoming chief in 1948, he and Violet moved to a westside address at **1155 West Fiftieth Avenue**. The house, while slightly more middle class, was certainly no palace. A plain weatherboard bungalow on a corner lot, it was far from the affluent houses of either McGeer or Celona, or as pleasant as Ray Munro's North Vancouver cottage. He said he loved sailing, but never had a boat. The only thing proven was that Mulligan had a mistress who lived on East Georgia Street in Strathcona. She testified that he paid for trips to the Okanagan, Vancouver Island, Montreal, and Seattle. She said Mulligan gave her a diamond ring, two large pieces of unset jade, a zircon ring, a Chinese teak chest and a typewriter. A *Province* headline of 1955 screamed, "Woman said Mulligan gave her $2,200 for love nest" in Langley, but couldn't explain why she sold it in 1952 for only five hundred dollars. Wearing a heavy disguise and identified as Helen Douglas, Mulligan's former mistress was careful in her testimony. When Tupper asked if Mulligan was receiving any money, she answered, "My impression was that he might have been … I guess there was some money being paid out, but I don't know to whom. It was his business, not mine."

Jack Whelan, an ex-cop, testified that when he and Mulligan were both detectives and partners, they investigated a break-in at a private home. Mulligan, he said, shoved a glass piggy bank full of coins into his coat and later split the proceeds, eleven dollars each, with Whelan. Whelan, an ex-wrestler, promoter, truck driver, and waiter wasn't the most credible of witnesses, but his brother Harry was and took the stand after Whelan. Harry Whelan testified that as Mulligan's deputy chief, he refused to take money from gamblers and it cost him a demotion to superintendent. Three hours before taking the stand for a second time, the fifty-three-year-old Harry Whelan took his thirty-eight revolver and shot himself in the chest at his **1325 East Seventeenth Street** home. He died in the same room, using the same gun that his father had used to kill himself years before. According to reports at the time, and to Bernie Smith who worked for Whelan, the shooting had nothing to do with police bribes, but was because he was afraid that personal information about his family would come out at trial and embarrass his wife and two young sons.

Chapter 4

ALVO VON ALVENSLEBEN: SECRET AGENT?

In 1906, Benjamin Franklin Dickens was one of dozens of men packed into the old O'Brien Hall at the corner of Homer and Hastings Streets in Vancouver. It was the first meeting of the Hundred Thousand Club, an early version of Tourism Vancouver. While the association had a mission and a slogan, "In 1910, Vancouver then will have 100,000 men," they badly need a leader.

Years later, Benny Franklin told City of Vancouver archivist Major Matthews, "No one seemed to know just how to get organized. A loud voice with a foreign accent called out from the back of the hall and moved that a chairman be elected. It was the voice of Alvo von Alvensleben. Soon after, he became a very active businessman in Vancouver."

It was certainly a turning point for Alvensleben. A reporter for *B.C. Magazine* wrote about the meeting, "A voice was heard addressing the chairman from a remote part of the hall, all heads turned. In a few minutes the meeting realized that it was listening to an organizer of marked ability. Under the guidance of that young man, their enthusiasm was crystallized, resolutions were passed, officers were appointed, rules were drawn up and the club was launched on a successful career. The young man who got them together was Alvo von Alvensleben. When the meeting was over, men pressed forward to congratulate the stranger. Little groups of twos and threes speculated upon who he was and from whence he had come."

Gustav Konstantin "Alvo" von Alvensleben lived in Vancouver less than a decade, yet his fingerprints are all over the city. He was a dashing Errol Flynn-like character, with a German accent and big dreams. When he hit his stride, he was unstoppable. He brought millions of dollars of German investment into Vancouver and bought up large tracts of land and huge houses. Before going fabulously broke in 1913, he had a personal fortune of around $25 million. His business interests included mining, forestry, and fishing. He

Alvo von Alvensleben, Portrait, Circa 1913
City of Vancouver Archives Photo # P1082
Photographer: George T. Wadds

financed the Dominion Trust Building in downtown Vancouver, at one point the tallest building in the British Empire, and it was Alvensleben's capital that built and developed the Wigwam Inn into a luxury resort.

Alvensleben remains an enigma. A capitalist, certainly, but his actions as a mine owner and his dealings with ordinary workers show he had an intriguing socialist bent and radical ideas for the time. And almost a century after he left Canada for Seattle, driven out by the war, no one really knows if he was a savvy businessman, a shady salesman, or a German James Bond.

Whoever he really was, Alvo von Alvensleben had a musical name that rolled easily off the tongue, and he was one of the biggest movers and shakers in early Vancouver. As the third son of a count, his father was at one time ambassador to the court of the Tsar, Alvensleben was a lieutenant in the Prussian army until March 1904, when he resigned his commission against the wishes of his father and, in his own words, "decided to do some pioneering in far-away countries."

While his penniless start makes great copy, he was hardly a rags-to-riches immigrant. He had the connections, the education, and the charm to convince people like Emma Mumm, the champagne heiress, Bertha Krupp, heir to the Krupp fortune, General von Mackensen, and even the Kaiser himself to open up their bank accounts.

Many differing stories about his background exist, but the best is from Alvensleben himself who, in 1939 and by then a U.S. citizen living in Seattle, wrote a long letter to the editor correcting an earlier article. He took issue when the reporter called him a "hobo."

He said, "It is true that I arrived in Vancouver, B.C. in June 1904 with less than four dollars in my pocket and within a very few days was pitching hay in Agassiz." He then described how he fished for the Brunswick Cannery. "I can assure the editor that the handling of a Columbia River gillnet boat and a few hundred fathoms of net is work, and very hard work," he wrote. "I have gambled a lot in my life—as stated in the article—and I have speculated with abandon, more particularly in the old days, but then a "boom" is as catching as the measles, and I have no doubt whatsoever that the old timers in Vancouver will heartily agree with me when I state that I was by no means the only one who caught it…This article closes with the statement that I went bankrupt before the war. It would have been more correct to state that the outbreak of the war broke me and my associates as completely as it broke thousands of others. Incidentally I never went through bankruptcy." The letter was signed Alvo von Alvensleben, 208 Columbia Street, Seattle.

The Vancouver of 1906 was a speculators paradise with great sums of money made from buying and selling land. Alvensleben, who by this time had managed to get seed money together from his various ventures, took out a full-page ad in the *Daily Province* promoting his real-estate company. It wasn't long before he'd convinced relatives and their associates to invest in the province's abundant natural resources. Not everyone was impressed. CPR president Thomas Shaughnessy called him a "hare-brained speculator, and nothing more."

Alvensleben was young, well connected, and shrewd. In 1907 he bought one of the first seats on the brand new Vancouver Stock Exchange for one hundred and twenty five dollars. The following year, the city directory listed A.V. Alvensleben as living at the tony Glencoe Lodge owned by B.T. Rogers on West Hastings Street. That July, he married Edith Mary Westcott who came from a well-connected local family.

By 1909, Alvensleben was one of Vancouver's best known business leaders. He advertised real estate deals from Lulu Island to Point Grey in the Lower Mainland and Stewart in northwestern B.C. He backed the two million dollar Vancouver docks proposal of 1909, which, had it gone through, would have seen eighteen wharves along Kitsilano Point built. His company advertisement now said: "Financial brokers, real estate, timber, mines, estate management, and rents collected."

Over the next few years, Alvensleben added more and more companies to his roster, mostly in real estate and timber. He was behind the Standard Fish and Fertilizer Company, the Vancouver-Nanaimo Coal Mining Company, the Vancouver Timber and Trading Company, Vancouver Springs and Indian River Park, the Piercite Powder Company, the Queen Charlotte Island Fisheries, and the German Canadian Trust. His company, Pacific Coast Fishing, built a three hundred thousand dollar cold-storage plant at Pacofi Bay in the Queen Charlottes.

In 1911 a reporter wrote, "His name on a prospectus has come to be recognized as a guarantee that it is a genuine proposition."

A half-page ad in the 1912 City Directory has Alvensleben as president of the Vancouver Timber Company. "Authorized capital ten million dollars, dealer in logs and timber lands. We are the owners of three billion feet of B.C. tidewater timber, crown grant and licenses. Will cut up in large or small blocks. Deal direct with responsible owners, principals only. Titles perfect. Terms liberal. 744 Hastings Street West." That year, he had fifty employees and, aside from timber, interests in fishing, mining, oil wells, real estate, and a trust company.

Alvensleben's personal properties grew. He owned a mansion in Kerrisdale and houses and property in North Vancouver, Pitt Meadows, and Issaquah Washington.

CROFTON HOUSE

Instead of following the rich to Shaughnessy Heights, in 1909 the Alvenslebens paid thirty thousand dollars for a house with twenty acres at **3200 West Forty-first Avenue** at the corner of Blenheim in Kerrisdale. Built in 1902 for Richard Byron Johnson, Alvensleben made a number of additions to the house and moved in the next year. He bought a string of thoroughbred horses, and by 1912, it took thirteen servants to run the household and cater the extravagant parties. Alvensleben was one of the first people to buy a motor car, and he and B.T. Rogers, another local millionaire, supposedly whipped around town in their Packard Tourers. Apparently, in Alvensleben's case, it was often with the chauffeur huddled in the back seat.

In 1931, Mr. Clampitts, a Kitsilano car conductor, told Vancouver archivist Major Matthews that he helped to build the streetcar line along Forty-first Avenue twenty years before. "At first we had a little 'dinky' car to Dunbar Street. It was a wild kind of place then, but these people who lived there were the kindest people I ever knew. I remember one time, it was Christmas, the folks brought us out a Christmas dinner and we, the conductor and I (the motorman) ate it in the car. They had it all fixed up on a silver tray, with white napkins, silver napkin rings, silver jugs, turkey dinners, and hot mince pies. On another Christmas we had five turkey dinners sent out to us by a resident along the streetcar line and we ate them in the car. I know I got twenty-eight cigars on one day, and the conductor got twenty-five. You remember Alvo von Alvensleben, the German friend of Kaiser Bill? Well Taylor, he ran the night shift, he never troubled to take lunch. Every night, they never missed, Alvensleben sent him out his lunch and a glass of wine."

Another night when the Alvensleben's threw a party, Alvensleben went out, stopped the tram, and invited all the passengers to the party. After eating and drinking, they hopped back on board and continued the trip.

In August 1913, the *Daily Province* wrote about the many cars "driven over the suburban roads," to a garden party held at Alvensleben's "country home." The guests played lawn tennis and the "novel entertainment" of clay pigeon shooting. "Dinner was served to the guests at seven o'clock and with the beginning of dusk the grounds were illuminated with Japanese lanterns swung in graceful lines among the trees and shrubbery and outlining the broad piazzas." *The Province* reporter wrote about the after-dinner dancing to two orchestras, and the impressive Parisian café in the garden.

The parties stopped suddenly at the outbreak of war in 1914. Alvensleben, in Germany at the time, read the signs and stayed in Seattle. The Custodian of Enemy Alien Property

CROFTON HOUSE SCHOOL — ALVENSLEBEN'S OLD RESIDENCE, CIRCA 1940.
PHOTO: COURTESY OF CROFTON HOUSE SCHOOL
ARCHIVES [94-P13.59, #3/10]

stripped him of all assets. Like many others in Vancouver caught by the downturn in the
economy, Alvensleben's $3.4 million debts way outstripped his one million dollar assets.

    According to a history of the Crofton House School by Elizabeth Bell-Irving, the
Kerrisdale house stood empty, neglected, and hopelessly entangled in legal wrangles until
1919 when it sold to Robert J. Cromie, publisher of *The Vancouver Sun*. The original
twenty acres had been reduced to about thirteen acres after the rest had been sold to pay
off Alvensleben's creditors. The Cromies fixed up the house and added an upstairs bedroom for their daughter. In 1942, Bernadette Cromie, now a widow, sold the house and
property to the Crofton House School for fifteen thousand dollars.

WIGWAM INN

Benny Dickens arrived in Vancouver from Belleville, Ontario in 1898 and joined the staff of the brand new *Daily Province* as the advertising manager. He worked there for a year then branched out into his own sign writing shop. In 1904 he had a West End address, the area where most of the rich lived, but instead of a mansion, his home was a modest house at **1101 Thurlow Street**, in the area now known as Mole Hill.

As people started to make bags of money in Vancouver's heady real-estate market, Dickens also saw his calling and added real-estate speculation and promotion to his portfolio. He bought two hundred acres of land at Indian River and in the *Daily Province*, announced his plan to build a large summer resort.

In June 1937, Dickens told Major Matthews that he sold his interest in *The World* (L.D. Taylor's newspaper) and joined the Royal Business Exchange as manager and vice-president. During that time, he heard about some land at Indian River. He said, "I met a man, John Bain, and he and I bought some property on Nineteenth in North Vancouver. Told me he had a piece of property to sell at Indian River, but that he was not the sort of man to push and promote it. 'I'll buy it myself!' and did so without even seeing it. I gave him a cheque right there and he drew from his pocket an old drawing that looked like one of those charts showing how to find lost treasure that you read about in magazines. It was of the location of the mineral spring near the mouth of the river."

Dickens plans were much larger than his wallet, and he soon ran out of capital. "I got busy and landscaped it myself, did all the design and everything up there is my work. I had twenty or forty men working. I had not enough dollars to carry on so Alvensleben bought a half interest and supplied the money," he told Matthews.

Dickens needed the cash, but obviously resented his partner. "It was Alvensleben this and Alvensleben that, but I did the work." He told Matthews that he hired Fred Townley, the architect that would design Vancouver's City Hall in 1936, to "improve on my sketch and the Wigwam Inn resulted."

Another bone of contention for Dickens was that Alvensleben had put the hotel license under his name. He said to Matthews, "I did not like that. My dear old mother would have turned in her grave if she had known I had the license to sell liquors."

Any respectable resort has to have residents and Alvensleben and Dickens sold fifty by one hundred foot lots for two hundred to three hundred dollars depending on their location. The terms were one hundred dollars cash and the balance paid at ten dollars a month. A 1907 magazine ad in *Saturday Sunset* had a sketch of the future hotel and a

WIGWAM INN, CIRCA 1913.
CITY OF VANCOUVER ARCHIVES, PHOTO #LGN 1028. PHOTOGRAPHER UNKNOWN.

flood of flowery copy. "There is really no scenic feature in America to compare with it. There is no such combination of wild grandeur and secluded reposeful beauty, no place where the sublime and gentle in creation mingle and blend, nowhere that one may so easily enjoy B.C. mountain scenery amid the comforts of a Sylvan home," it waxed on. "From the verandah of a summer home in these surroundings a businessman need be no further away from his office than thousands of men who daily journey from suburban homes in New York, Boston and other cities in stifling dust and enervating heat." The company, said the ad, would operate a private boat service to Vancouver, guaranteed to get business people to the office by 9:00 A.M.

The Wigwam Inn began construction in 1909. The following June, the owners invited six hundred carefully handpicked guests to sail up Indian Arm in the "Baramba" for the Grand Opening of the Inn. The promotion cost a whopping one thousand dollars but was likely cheap not only for the publicity it generated, but also for the lots it sold on that day.

Alvensleben changed the theme from Indian to German and billed the Inn as a "Luftkurot," meaning a fresh-air resort. Guests wandered through beautifully land-scaped gardens along paths that led to forest. At night they ate sausages and drank beer while bands oompah-pahed German songs. Four different sternwheelers ferried guests up and down from Vancouver who paid three dollars and fifty cents a day to stay at the Inn. On April 8, 1911, American millionaires John D. Rockefeller and John Jacob Astor signed the guest book. Astor died a year later aboard the Titanic.

When the war hit, the rich and famous stopped coming to the Wigwam Inn, and Alvensleben left for Seattle. The government seized the Inn in 1914 and it sold to Wisconsin timber baron E.J. Young the following year. Young was attracted more to the forest than the resort. He ditched the German theme, and after he died, the Inn changed hands several times and all but disappeared from public view until 1961. That year, two boat loads of RCMP officers uncovered an illegal gambling operation complete with equipment, booze, and what they thought were plates for printing counterfeit money.

Other owners tried to breathe new life into the Inn. According to a 1980 *Globe and Mail* article, in 1972 Tony Casano paid one hundred and fifty thousand dollars for the Inn and one hundred and fifty five acres. He sold it a few years later to a group of local businessman for five hundred thousand dollars. Then, in 1985, the Royal Vancouver Yacht Club bought the Inn. Now, it's strictly members only.

NORTH VANCOUVER

Alvensleben's name is linked to properties in Stewart, B.C., on Vancouver Island and, closer to home, to a North Vancouver hunting lodge, a Pitt Meadows house and acreage, and a stately Port Mann home. Most of the associations are anecdotal, and it's impossible to tell if he actually lived at or even visited these properties, but the stories continue.

His name is attached to a 1912 hunting lodge at **437 Somerset Street** in North Vancouver. The first house built in the area, it sits on a high piece of property near the top of the Twenty-ninth Street hill overlooking Burrard Inlet. It would have been surrounded by forest at the time and very grand with its wraparound veranda and a circular carriage drive.

The city directories list a Baron Lubbwitz living in the house in 1913 and then no one until 1929 when J. Gillespie, an inspector with Excelsior Life, lived there until 1931. Alvensleben's main residence was in Kerrisdale, so it's quite likely that a fellow German lived at the hunting lodge. As a German-owned property, the government probably seized the house under the Custodian of Enemy Alien Property.

Between 1931 and 1933 the Somerset house was rented out to the Drainie family and plays a small role in Bronwyn Drainie's biography of her father, Canadian actor John Drainie. "Now this was a house," writes Bronwyn Drainie. "Big enough to have its own billiard room, it was also perfectly designed for putting on plays because the living room opened onto an enormous front hall through a pair of sliding doors." One Christmas when her father was about twelve he directed a production of *Twelfth Night*, writes Drainie.

Senator Raymond Perrault and his wife Barbara Perrault, a City of North Vancouver councillor and a member of the Heritage Advisory Committee, lived at 437 Somerset from 1974 until 1995. Barbara Perrault says there were official wax seals on all the windows that dated back to the First World War when the federal government had impounded the house. She added that there are enough design similarities in the five thousand square foot house to link it to the much larger Wigwam Inn.

For years people talked of a secret radio room and tunnels leading from the cellar of the Somerset Street house. Supposedly, a gardener found one some years later. Fran Gundry calls these notions "hysterical war rumours." Gundry's father, a psychiatrist, bought the house in 1945. She says it was a great house to grow up in, and after her father died, her mother lived there until 1972. "We heard there were tunnels," she says. "We were always looking for tunnels." But they never found any.

PITT MEADOWS

Donald Luxton is a historian and author who has documented heritage houses for a number of municipalities in Greater Vancouver. He worked on the heritage inventory for both the City of North Vancouver and Pitt Meadows and says that while there is slim evidence connecting Alvensleben to the Somerset house, it's well documented that he owned substantial amounts of property in Pitt Meadows.

Unlike other houses Alvensleben owned that were built in elevated locations with water views, the house at 14776 Harris Road in Pitt Meadows rests on the flats of Pitt Meadows between the Pitt and Alouette Rivers. The dilapidated house has Edwardian features and Craftsman-style details such as the exposed rafters and remnants of a wraparound verandah. Luxton says an interesting similarity between the Pitt Meadows and North Vancouver houses is that both have wall dormers with jerkin-headed roofs. Luxton says Alvensleben never lived in the Pitt Meadows house and thinks it was likely built as a caretaker's residence. After war broke out, rumours abounded that the Pitt Meadows house, the North Vancouver hunting lodge, and Baron Carl von Mackensen's house in Port Kells were used for spying activities where secret signals passed by mirror between the three houses.

SURREY

Alvensleben's name pops up again at Port Kells and Port Mann in Surrey, but again it's hard to pin down exactly what he owned, if anything, and when. There is some confusion between Alvensleben and a fellow German, Mackensen, a friend of his who, in 1910, bought a house at **9564 192nd Street**, at the corner of Ninety-sixth Avenue in Port Kells. Locals dubbed it the "Castle" because of the turreted tower Mackensen built on the south side. It had a stained glass window depicting the family coat of arms, a foyer with standing suits of armour, and swords, pistols, and muskets hanging on the walls.

The Baron made himself popular by throwing huge Christmas parties at the castle every year, inviting everyone in the area, serving drinks and food and giving everybody gifts.

"This was really a highlight of the Christmas season for the few years the Baron was there," says Kay Kells.

Kells, whose family has lived in the area since the late 1800s, has extensively researched and written about the area. Over the years, she's recorded interviews with some of the earliest settlers who remember both Alvensleben and Mackensen. "Alvensleben owned some property next door to Baron von Mackensen on the east side," she says. "It was the beginning of the 1900s, and he had an old shack with four walls and a bit of a roof. I don't know whether he stayed there, and I imagine it was confiscated during the war."

As for Mackensen, when World War One broke out, his popularity took a sharp nose dive. Using incredibly bad judgment, in an environment already thick with fear and paranoia, he flew the German flag from his roof top. Kells says this incensed the locals, already scared of a German invasion, and a few, including her father-in-law Fred Kells, told him to take down the flag or they would shoot it down.

"The authorities searched the home several times to see if there was anything subversive going on, and according to my mother-in-law, a young constable found papers and a map hidden in the dirt of a plant holder. He went through that and found places marked on the map, of which Germans were going to get these different properties around Port Kells when they won the war."

Unfortunately, nobody can remember actually seeing this map, or what happened to it. Evidence seized from suspected spies was lost in a government office fire in the 1960s. In January 1915, Mackensen ended up in an internment camp in Vernon as a supposed employee of Kaiser Wilhelm II. Kells says that her father-in-law was a guard there, which must have made for interesting conversations after the flag episode. Evidence was flimsy, so it's hard to say if he had the wherewithal to spy for Germany, but because he was the nephew of General August von Mackensen, he spent over four years in the camp.

According to a story in the *Surrey Leader* in 2005, before coming to Canada, Mackensen spent a few lacklustre years in the German military and married a rich heiress in 1902. Supposedly, her mother paid him the equivalent of two hundred and fifty thousand Canadian dollars to divorce her daughter and hit the road. He took the cash, arranged an honourable discharge from the army in 1904, and headed for Canada. The Baron's choice of the farming community of Port Kells was rather odd, but most likely it allowed him to stretch his windfall and let him live a sort of feudal lord existence, which must have appealed to his aristocratic nature.

After the war ended, the government booted Mackensen out of the country. He made several attempts to get back an estimated two hundred thousand dollars in confiscated assets. A story in the *Surrey Leader* says that in 1967 the Canadian Government released thirty five dollars worth of stock. Mackensen died in Astfeld, Germany in 1967. Now called "Spy House" by the locals, rumour has it that the Baron had a clandestine short-wave radio in a secret room of the house and that he spied on ships along the Fraser River.

The Castle changed hands a number of times, running for a few years as an alternative school. In 2004, the City of Surrey rather aptly approved the rezoning of the Castle into a pub and liquor store.

Pillath House, another Surrey property at **11113 - 148**th **Street** in Port Mann, is also linked to Alvensleben. A Victorian with Queen Anne details, the house sits far back from the street on a huge lot and looks out onto the Fraser River. The original owners, Ludwig Pillath and his wife Wilemena, were originally from Prussia and that's probably the connection with Alvensleben. They operated a sawmill in Kentucky and arrived in Surrey in 1903 where they took up farming. Ludwig died in 1918 and Wilemena sold the property to her daughter Emma Pillath Coffin, but continued to live there until her death in 1963. The City of Surrey bought the property in 1990.

WASHINGTON STATE

It may be that Alvensleben saw the writing on the real-estate wall, or that he cleverly diversified his investments, in any case, he acquired substantial coal holdings on Vancouver Island and later south of the border in Issaquah, Washington. Stephen Hume writes in the July 31, 2004 issue of *The Vancouver Sun*, "His influence was astonishing. When German chemical industries ran short of high-grade carbon, Alvensleben quickly located a source in Washington State and then, after a quick trip to Berlin, came up with a million to invest in developing the Issaquah Mine."

"Coal," writes Hume, "was the strategic military commodity in 1914 that oil is today. Indeed, the German squadron's secret movements in the Pacific were predicated upon where the cruisers could obtain coal."

In 1913, Alvensleben took the million he'd raised and bought the surface and coal rights to about two thousand acres for the Issaquah and Superior Coal Mining Company. He installed tunnels, gangways, tracks, and surface equipment, and spent one hundred thousand dollars on modern machinery for grading and cleaning the coal.

Surprisingly, considering his privileged upbringing and arrogant demeanour, Alvensleben brought some radical ideas to mining. He built decent houses for the miners, paid them a reasonable wage, and wasn't afraid of the labour unions. He argued that any industry that couldn't pay fairly and offer humane hours didn't have the right to exist.

The plant was capable of producing two thousand tons of coal a day. In 1913, plans were in the works to develop fire clay deposits, install a briquette plant, and a plant to manufacture commercial fertilizer. More than five hundred men worked at the mine in this first stage, and Alvensleben oversaw a monthly payroll of thirty thousand dollars. More homes and business buildings went up at Issaquah that year than in the preceding twenty years.

Rumours swirled that the Kaiser himself had invested in the plant. In 1928 Alvensleben told a reporter, "I wish to deny unequivocally that the Kaiser ever had money invested in the Issaquah mine. Any funds the Emperor had for investment were placed by two conservative Jewish banking houses in Berlin. Struggling mines on the western shore of North America were not on the list of these bankers."

Alvensleben built a house in Issaquah set on five acres of land just off Wildwood Boulevard and made entirely of fir using tongue and groove construction. The site is now full of condominiums, but in 1977, current owners moved Alvensleben's house to Gilman Village as part of a shopping centre. Locals still call the house "Alien Acres." The

Taylor family of Issaquah bought the house in 1944, and many others lived in the home over the years.

Once the war kicked in, the government sold the mine property to the Pacific Coast Coal Company for a little over three hundred thousand dollars. Alvensleben, unable to continue his mining operations, took up real estate in Seattle.

When the U.S. joined the war in 1917, Alvensleben was branded as a spy, some even called him the "Kaiser's secret agent." The Americans unceremoniously shipped him off to an internment camp in Fort Douglas, Utah for the next four years.

Back in Vancouver, his spectacular rise and crashing fall made Alvensleben even more controversial. Rumours abounded about gun emplacements at Alvensleben's Kerrisdale house and tunnels that supposedly led to the river. These rumours swirled around for years, including one about a secret radio room in the North Vancouver house and a submarine base at the Pacofi Bay, site of his Pacific Coast fishing company. Nothing was ever found.

THE CRASH

One of the major turning points in the fortunes of Vancouver was the collapse of the Dominion Trust in 1914. Up until its demise at the end of that year, the Dominion Trust was one of the most influential corporate concerns in the province, with the office tower—still standing on West Hastings Street—as a corporate symbol of its prosperity. Before the crash, the Trust had assets of five million dollars. It had expanded from a small local firm to a national company with branches in B.C., the Prairie Provinces, and Prince Edward Island.

Any doubt that the company was in over its thirteen-storey head in speculative lending practices in real estate and questionable loans stopped on October 12, 1914. William Arnold, the company's vice-president and general manager, killed himself with a shotgun in his Shaughnessy Heights garage. Before the end of that month, the Dominion Trust closed its doors with debts of more than two million dollars. According to Michael Kluckner in *Vancouver: The Way it Was*, a debt of $1,143,000 was included in the balance sheet, incurred by Alvensleben, who was temporarily residing in Seattle.

His Canadian assets seized by the government and sold off to pay debt, Alvensleben continued working in real estate in Seattle, living and dealing in far more modest circumstances than he'd left behind in Vancouver. The Alvensleben's had three children:

Margaret, Gero, and Bodo, all born in Canada. Margaret died in 2004, but was close to her nephew Brian Alvensleben and often conveyed to him what little she knew of the family history. Margaret was eight when the Alvenslebens fled Canada, and she remembered the affluence of the Kerrisdale days. She told Brian that when they left Canada, they took as much money, jewellery, and small valuables that they were able to fit into the car. They moved into a house on N.E. Forty-fourth Street in Laurelhurst, an affluent residential neighbourhood by the University of Washington. The family lived frugally during Alvensleben's four years in the internment camp, surviving off the money they made selling off the jewellery and what they'd been able to salvage from Canada.

"He came to Seattle and worked in real-estate development, but never made it big again," says Brian Alvensleben. "When I knew him, he was pretty bitter. You see those movies about Germany and they have some German count or noble person—that's just what he looked like, just what he acted like. He was extremely good looking, even in his late 70s and early 80s, and I remember him as being kind of austere."

Brian says his grandfather was a strict disciplinarian. He hated the stories reporters had made up about him in Canada and was furious when Margaret decided to study journalism at the University of Washington, disowning her for a period of time.

"She was a fascinating woman," says Brian of Margaret. "She was the first woman editor of the *University of Washington Daily* and the first female hard-news reporter on the *Seattle Times*." Briefly married to a judge in Ottawa, Margaret divorced and married William Newcombe, a well-known Canadian abstract artist, and lived with him in Portugal and Mexico. Brian's father, Gero, was educated as an electrical engineer at the University of Washington and worked for contractors in Seattle and Alaska and later as a salesman for Westinghouse Electric. Bodo, the youngest son, fought with the American Regiment on Normandy Beach in World War Two. He was a construction worker and an alcoholic with a genius IQ, says Brian.

Long after the war ended, Alvensleben took a few trips up to British Columbia. On one in 1963, he had a friend take him up to the Wigwam Inn in his boat. He turned to the friend and said, "I must have been crazy."

Alvensleben died two years later in Seattle. He vehemently denied all reports of spying for the Germans.

Chapter 5

THE WEST END

In April 1996, The Residences on Georgia went up for sale. A couple of hundred people snaked in a line from Jervis almost back to Bute Street to get a glimpse of Canada's latest $115 million condo project. That the two, thirty-seven-storey towers wouldn't be built for another two years didn't seem to faze them, they were happy to wait up to forty-five minutes for a look at a model, a display suite, and some high-tech equipment. If they wandered to the corner of Jervis Street they could see Harry Abbott's turn of the century mansion. Soon to be lavished with a $3.2 million renovation, this house, the last on Blue Blood Alley, would turn into five modern condo units. In exchange for saving this piece of history, the City of Vancouver gave the developers the go-ahead to build two extra floors on each tower as their heritage density bonus. And even before the hammer fell, four of the five future Abbott House units sold between $185,000 and $378,000 as part of the pre-sale blitz.

The West End is once again a desired place to live, not just for office workers who can live near their work, but for the retired and for the rich who can afford to shell out millions for a Georgia Street penthouse. Starting around 1884, when it was clear that the Canadian Pacific Railway would bypass Port Moody in favour of a Coal Harbour terminus, the West End has been in a constant state of reinvention. The CPR was the first real estate developer and sold expensive homes to the wealthy and the wannabes. As a young city, it was all about where you worked, the CPR or the Bank of Montreal for instance, or what you did, real-estate development or lumber, that put you on the top of the elite heap. Connections got you memberships in the snobby Vancouver Club, the Terminal City Club, and front seats at the Opera House. Tennis, horse riding and sailing clubs also catered to the wealthy.

A book with the unlikely title of the *Vancouver Elite Directory*, published in 1908 said eighty-six percent of those who rated a listing lived in the West End, while six percent lived downtown and the rest were scattered throughout Point Grey, Kitsilano, and Fairview, with a few holdouts still in the East End.

Henry Braithwaite Abbott (H.B.), general superintendent for the CPR, was one of the West End's first residents. When his CPR-built mansion went up at the corner of Howe and Hastings, a stampede of CPR heavyweights such as Henry Cambie, namesake of Cambie Street, Alfred Graham Ferguson, CPR engineer and chair of the first Park's Board (Ferguson Point in Stanley Park is named after him), and Dr. J.M. Lefevre, CPR doctor and real estate developer, followed to the exclusive new area.

H.B. was one of four CPR directors present at Craigellachie, now a tourist stop between Salmon Arm and Revelstoke on the Trans-Canada Highway, to watch Sir Donald Smith drive in the last spike on November 7, 1885. He was behind the subdivision of the original Vancouver town site and had blue-chip connections. His brother Sir John J. Abbott served as Prime Minister in 1891 and 1892, and as part of his role with the CPR (and through notable family connections), H.B. entertained famous tourists in his home such as Francis Ferdinand, the Archduke of Austria (assassinated in 1914), Sir Henry Stanley, explorer and author, Edward Blake, leader of the federal Liberal Party and Sir Robert Baden Powell. Local bankers and railway tycoons like William Van Horne, Lord Shaughnessy, and Donald Smith (Lord Strathcona) also showed up on the guest list. When H.B. retired at the end of the century, he built the home at **720 Jervis Street,** the first, and now last, remaining mansion left along the section of Georgia Street once called Blue Blood Alley.

BLUE BLOOD ALLEY

The most startling thing about the six thousand square foot Abbott house, aside from the fact that it still exists, is that it sits smack in the middle of a sea of steel and glass fronted condominiums. The house is now painted CPR red in honour of its first inhabitant and still has high ceilings, and beautiful bay and stained glass windows. The largest stained glass window on the Jervis Street side is a massive work created by the Bloomfields. H.B. Abbott is the Abbott in Abbotsford and also gave his name to Abbott Street, one of the first four streets in Vancouver that runs through the Downtown Eastside. Its only connection to blue blood is that it crosses "Blood Alley" in Gastown. Abbott lived at the Jervis Street house until his death in 1915. He left an estate worth over $200,000. According to *The Vancouver Sun's* John Mackie, Abbott mansion became a rooming house and was later converted to apartments when the family sold it in 1942 for $5,500.

As the bluebloods left the alley in the early years of the twentieth century for higher ground above English Bay, mansions started springing up along Harwood, Burnaby, and Davie Streets. These years toward the end of the 1890s and the early years of the next century played out like an Ethel Wilson novel. Accounts of the time have the wealthy flitting from manor to manor, presenting calling cards, and sipping on lemonade while playing croquet and badminton on manicured lawns.

In 1949, Ethel Wilson wrote the *Innocent Traveller*, a largely autobiographical book about an orphaned girl coming to live in the West End of Vancouver in the late 1890s. "The West End was wooded," she writes. "The houses all had wooden trimmings and verandahs, and on the verandah steps when day was done the families came out and sat and talked and counted the box pleats on the backs of fashionable girls' skirts as they went by; and visitors came and sat and talked, and idly watched the people too, and watched the mountains. And then they all went in and made a cup of cocoa. It was very pleasant and there seemed to be no trouble anywhere upon the face of the earth that you could discern."

In the novel, the orphaned girl lived on Barclay Street with her grandmother. In reality, Wilson's grandmother was Annie Malkin, mother of wholesale grocer and later mayor, William H. Malkin. According to city directories, in 1905 Ann Elizabeth Malkin lived on Barclay Street, so it's likely Ethel also lived there in the early 1900s. At least in the 1901 census, Ann, sixty-eight is listed as household head with her brother Wilcox Edge, fifty-seven, sisters Anne, fifty-four, and Eliza Edge, fifty-six, sons William, thirty-two, and Philip, twenty-three, granddaughter Ethel Bryant (Wilson), thirteen, and the cook, Ho Yew, twenty.

From the early 1940s, Ethel lived with her husband Dr. Wallace Wilson at the elegant Kensington Place apartments at number **42-1386 Nicola Street** at the corner of Beach Avenue. Phillip Julien, the architect behind Riffington, one of the largest homes ever built in Victoria, designed the apartment building in 1912. Painted yellow with white trim and blue window frames, the apartments would look right at home in sun drenched Spain or Italy. According to a biography of Wilson, the couple lived in relative luxury, "surrounded by oriental rugs, books, a photo of a sketch of Winston Churchill, an original Burne-Jones pencil drawing, and the same housekeeper for twenty-two years. Ethel Wilson claimed to have written her first stories in the late 1930s in the family car while her husband did house calls." Apparently, Wilson both knew and influenced the later writings of Margaret Laurence and Alice Munro. She also took painting lessons from Emily Carr.

Another famous British Columbian, William John Bowser, lived at Edgehill at **1225 Harwood Street** on the slope above Beach Avenue. Now rundown and in need of a coat of paint, the rather plain cream and brown trim house with a massively large front yard still has a magnificent view of English Bay. Bowser, born in 1867 in New Brunswick, moved to Vancouver after graduating with a law degree from Dalhousie. Elected MLA in 1903, he served until 1924. As a lawyer, he defended a bunch of degenerates, and in 1907 became Attorney General. By 1912 Bowser lived in Victoria in a three-storey mansion designed by Samuel Maclure. He had also acquired a reputation as the "Napoleon of politics" because he was a tad brusque, didn't like to compromise, and looked uncannily like the infamous general. The attitude didn't hurt his rise in politics because in 1915 Bowser became Premier of B.C. The party was defeated the following year and he led the opposition party until 1924. He died from a heart attack at the Hotel Vancouver in 1933 while campaigning for a provincial election. His death, according to a front page story in *The Province* was due to "overstrain caused by the excitement of the campaign."

Two blocks down at **1492 Harwood**, James and Helen Gregory MacGill built a mustard-coloured house in 1908. Born in Hamilton, Ontario in 1864, Helen was the first woman to graduate from Toronto's University of Trinity College. She first worked as a reporter and later as the first woman judge in B.C. From 1917 she presided over Vancouver's Juvenile Court, fighting for the rights of women and children throughout her illustrious career. The MacGill's youngest daughter, Elsie, became the first woman to graduate in engineering at the University of Toronto and the first to take a master's degree in aeronautics at the University of Michigan in 1929. During World War Two she supervised the engineering work in the production of Hawker Hurricane fighters, the aircraft made famous through the Battle of Britain.

When the MacGills moved into their new house, it had a billiard room in the basement and out back, chickens and a kitchen garden, which Lee Wa Kee, the Chinese help, cultivated. The MacGill house is still there, now a strata conversion painted a regal red. At the side you can see an odd pattern of bricks on the chimney. The bricks, says the current owner, came from the Gastown fire.

The MacGill's finances went up and down with the times. James, a barrister who worked for Carter-Cotton's *Vancouver News Advertiser* when times were tough, had chunks of investment properties in Shaughnessy Heights and the West End. But after the bottom blew out of the real-estate market in 1913, the MacGills lost the Harwood Street house at a government tax sale and moved to rented digs on Nelson Street. By 1926, Helen MacGill's judge's salary had increased to one hundred dollars a month, and that same year, she received three thousand dollars in damages from an accident settlement. The MacGills were finally able to buy back the Harwood Street house. Their oldest daughter married there shortly after, and they lived there for another ten years until they traded down to a smaller house on Cardero Street. By 1945, the city directories have 1492 Harwood listed just as Columbus Lodge Rooms.

GABRIOLA

Benjamin Tingley Rogers, Vancouver's first millionaire industrialist, known as the Sugar King, built Gabriola at **1531 Davie Street** in 1900 for $25,000, about twice as much as the next best-dressed mansion in town. Designed by architect to the rich Samuel Maclure, at one time the mansion occupied the entire block with stables, outbuildings, and greenhouses. The mansion had eighteen fireplaces and, not to be outdone by Harry Abbott, stained glass in the entrance and several other panes, all created by the Bloomfields. The house got its name from the green sandstone on the outside that was quarried on Gabriola Island. Just past the threshold is a tile inset with the word "Angus," the maiden name of Mary Rogers. A major event in the city, *The Province* newspaper gave the August housewarming a huge write-up in the morning paper. "A successful dance was given by Mrs. B.T. Rogers on Friday evening at her handsome new stone residence on Davie Street. The floral decorations and many bright electric lights and the gay colours of the women's gowns made a festive scene," wrote the reporter. "In the small hours the guests departed after having sung 'For They are Jolly Good Fellows'." More interesting is Mary Rogers' diary entry. It says simply: "Housewarming. Nobody wanted to go at three in the morning. Mayor Townley made a ghastly speech."

Ten years later, Gabriola had lost its novelty for B.T. After returning from a trip to England, he started looking for a chunk of land on which to build a grand English-style manor and garden—bigger and better than the Davie Street mansion. The following year he bought ten acres from dairy farmer William Shannon at Granville and Fifty-seventh Avenue (what's now **7255 Granville Street**) and built a Beaux-Arts-style home that he called Shannon. Shannon itself, the coach house, and the gate house are now apartments, but much of the beautiful grounds remain, including fish ponds and landscaping. The original property stretched from Granville and Fifty-seventh Avenue to Adera and Fifty-fourth Avenue; but Shannon has met the fate of other large properties, and apartment buildings now ring the grounds.

Unfortunately for B.T., he died from a cerebral hemorrhage in 1918 at age fifty-two, never getting to spend time by any one of the multiple fireplaces. Mary, busy rearing seven children, took until 1925 to finish the house. By the time it was finished, Shannon had buildings for farm animals, a formal garden, a vegetable garden, and plenty of room to house twelve staffers and play host to many elegant parties.

Mary Rogers kept the house until 1936 and then moved to 3637 Angus Drive. Austin C. Taylor, president of Bralorne gold mine—one of the few stars in B.C.'s poor economy— paid $105,600 for the Shannon mansion. Taylor lived there until his death in 1965. Developer Peter Wall bought Shannon and hired architect Arthur Erickson to turn the property into a housing development.

As for Gabriola, after Mary left in the '20s, the house was converted into the Angus Apartments, probably to help finance the building of Shannon. City directories show that Charles Bentall, manager of Dominion Construction, the company that poured the foundation for Shannon in 1914, and his wife Edna, took apartment #206 at Gabriola in the 1930s. Bentall oversaw the development of the Bentall Centre in the 1960s and was a Canadian Business Hall of Fame inductee in 1986. Gabriola went into the restaurant business in 1978, first as Hy's Mansion and since 1993 under the Romano's Macaroni Grill banner.

MOLE HILL

Another area of the West End left largely intact, more by accident than plan, and swarming with social history is Mole Hill. Tucked in behind St. Paul's Hospital opposite Nelson Park, twenty-six heritage houses, now city owned, stretch in a square along Comox, Bute, Thurlow, and Pendrell Streets. The area, its name sounding like it came straight from the pages of *Wind in the Willows,* is actually named after Henry Mole, who moved to Comox Street after he retired from farming the land that is now the Point Grey Golf and Country Club in Southlands below South West Marine Drive. Anything left of his house, which was at 1025 Comox Street, now sits under the hospital.

1173 Pendrell Street towers above a white picket fence and a neatly trimmed hedge. Now painted in a plum colour with green trim, the rather plain Queen Anne house is one of the few houses in the area sitting on a full city lot. It first belonged to William A. Bauer, a provincial land surveyor, in 1898. Bauer only lived in the house for three years before moving to Seaton Street (now West Hastings) and sold the Comox Street house to Alexander Bethune, a contractor and builder who was Vancouver's mayor from 1907 to

HENRY MOLE RESIDENCE, 1025 COMOX STREET (NOW DEMOLISHED). YEAR: 1895.
CITY OF VANCOUVER ARCHIVES. PHOTO # BuP697
PHOTOGRAPHER: NORMAN CAPLE

1908. Bethune, who was born in Peterborough, Ontario in 1852, also had a brief stay in the house before he and his wife Mary Catherine McIntosh and their two daughters, Catherine and Alice, moved up the road to 1346 Pendrell in 1905. The next owner, Saul Grier Starratt, managed the New England Fish Company. Born in Nova Scotia in 1865, he arrived in B.C. in 1886. His wife Annie lived there until 1918.

Beautifully painted and preserved heritage houses line one side of the 1100 block of Pendrell Street. Public walkways full of shrubs and flowers spill over into lanes that wander between the houses and offer a great vantage point to check out more of the architecture and the gardens. Further down at **1117 Pendrell** near Thurlow, is a funky little Queen Anne peeking out from behind the back of some larger houses. This small house originally sat behind the George Leslie House at **1380 Hornby Street**. It was moved to Mole Hill in 2002. Leslie, a contractor/plasterer, was evidently good at his job, because he built a two-storey Queen Anne house complete with bay window, jigsaw balcony, and porch in 1889 and the smaller lane house in 1901. The Leslie family lived at the Hornby Street address until 1947 when it became Leslie House Ltd., an interior decorating business until 1966. Dress designers took the house over until 1973. The Hornby Street house is one of the oldest in the city and can be checked out for the price of an elegant plate of linguine alfredo and chardonnay. Umberto Menghi bought it and turned it into Il Giardino in 1973.

It's definitely worth a stroll along Comox Street, which runs opposite Nelson Park. Period homes line the entire 1100 block. The Mole Hill Child Care Centre at 1164 Comox was first owned by Francis Bowser, a shipping agent for the Dominion Customs Service. He is listed in the city directory with the delightful title of "chief landing waiter customs."

Bowser invested heavily and wisely in real estate and, after retiring in 1907, built the first home in the wilds of Kerrisdale at what is now Forty-fifth Avenue and MacDonald. The three-storey house once contained a ballroom with an Australian mahogany floor and a billiards room. In 1930 it was torn down and the property sold for $2,400. Bowser served as Reeve of Point Grey from 1910 to 1911. The older brother to former B.C. Premier, William Bowser, Francis married Jessie, daughter of William Sinclair a retired Hudson's Bay official, and they had five children. He's the Bowser behind the Bowser Block at Forty-first Avenue and West Boulevard in Kerrisdale.

BARCLAY SQUARE

Barclay Square is a designated heritage area bounded by Haro, Broughton, Barclay and Nicola Streets and filled with nine heritage homes. The oldest, dating back to 1890, gives a sense of the turn of the century Vancouver. These heritage houses are a mixture of elaborate Queen Anne Revival and Edwardian Builder styles, painted in heritage colours of mud yellows, blues, and greys. As a bonus, many of the trees are original.

The three houses on Barclay Street are the most magnificent of the lot. Thanks to some smart thinking and fancy footwork by the Community Arts Council of Vancouver, the 1893 Roedde House at **1415 Barclay**, is now a designated heritage house and museum open to public snooping. Like most, the house takes its name from its first occupant, Gustav Adolph Roedde, a German-born bookbinder and founder of the first bookbinding and printing company in the city. His wife Matilda and, at different times, their six children and three St. Bernards lived in the house until 1925. When the family's Christmas tree burst into flames in January 1913, the house was saved by the firemen working at the city's 1906 Firehall a block south on Nicola Street.

In 1943, Bill Roedde, son of Gustav Roedde, talked to Major Matthews at the City of Vancouver Archives about growing up in the West End. He told a story about playing in a sand pile at the corner of Barclay and Nicola Streets when he was a small boy in 1904. He heard a car spluttering down the street—a very rare occurrence at that time—and ran out to take a look. The driver, B.T. Rogers, the wealthy founder of B.C. Sugar with a reputation of being a bit of a speed freak, lost control of the car in the sand and ran over the boy's foot. Fortunately, the accident didn't do much damage to either boy or car, and B.T. cranked the car up, threw the boy onto the seat and drove him home. Bill, apparently, was so excited to be one of the first kids in the city to get a ride in a car that he hardly noticed the pain.

Around the mid-1920s, Gustav Roedde's thoughts turned to retirement. The family didn't much like the way the neighbourhood was changing from stately homes to apartment buildings and headed off to a house on Drummond Drive in Point Grey. They sold the Barclay Street house to James Blayney for $6,000, who then sold it in 1928 to H.W. Jeffrey, a local butcher, and his wife Clara. After Jeffrey died in 1935, his son-in-law Harry Oehlerking and his wife Helen ran a boarding house from the home. Roedde House remained a boarding house until the city bought it in 1966.

Today Roedde House is a magnificent specimen of Queen Anne architecture that stands in the midst of a large mature garden crowned by a beautiful magnolia tree and gazebo. The house is likely the design of Victoria architect Francis Mawson Rattenbury, a family friend from the Roeddes' stay in Victoria. Rattenbury would have been around twenty-five at the time and is the architect behind the Parliament Buildings, the Empress Hotel, and the Crystal Gardens in Victoria and a number of banks and court houses in B.C. Rattenbury is notorious, not for his architecture, but for his 1935 murder in England by his young wife, Alma Pakenham, and her lover, George Stoner. Stoner was sentenced to life imprisonment and was later released, while Pakenham was acquitted and soon after committed suicide.

Next door to Roedde House is a quirky little park that sits in a square of green grass behind a stone fence. An old sycamore maple and a row of Cappadocian maples lining the street have survived since the 1890s. Next to the park, Barclay Manor at **1477 Barclay Street** was the first house built on the street in 1890 for Charles Tetley, a mining engineer and city accountant, and his wife, Lucy. In 1905, the house sold to Frank Baynes, owner of the Dominion Hotel in Gastown. Baynes added a large hospital building to the north side of the house, which became Miss Clermont's West End Hospital and where the Roeddes' granddaughters were born. From 1919 to 1926 the house became a residence for Catholic girls called Rosary Hall, and in 1926, the house got the unlikely name of Barclay Manor when it became a boarding house for men. The cost for a week was twenty-three dollars shared or thirty dollars for a single room with two meals a day and maid service. Barclay Manor has housed the West End Senior's Network Society since 1990.

Around the corner on Broughton Street, three identical wooden houses with bay windows and large porches were designed around 1902 by architect Bedford Davidson. One of these, at **883 Broughton,** was home to Margaret MacLean, wife of Malcolm MacLean, Vancouver's first mayor. During his tenure, MacLean presided over the Great Fire in 1886. He died in 1895. The most famous visitor to the house was Canadian poet Robert Service, long before he'd even thought of either *The Cremation of Sam McGee* or *The Shooting of Dan McGrew.*

Service arrived in Vancouver dead broke around the early years of the Twentieth Century. He worked for a while on a farm in Duncan before getting a job as a clerk for the Canadian Bank of Commerce in Victoria. Constance MacLean, Margaret's daughter, met Service while working as a governess, and according to love letters found stashed away in a dresser drawer after she died in 1960, Service and MacLean had a six-year love affair. Service dedicated his first volume of poetry *Songs of a Sourdough* to C.M. In 1908 he vowed he would marry her if the bank didn't forbid employees earning less than $1,300 a year from marrying. But the letters stopped in 1908, and both Service and MacLean married other people. The remains of Sarah Emily Service, Robert's mother, lie in the Mountain View Cemetery in Vancouver.

It is remarkable how many mansions, early apartment buildings, and architecturally interesting heritage homes still exist in the West End. Until the mid 1950s, the tallest building in the West End was the eight-storey Sylvia Hotel. When the City of Vancouver decided to increase the population density in the area during this period, developers built more than two hundred and twenty high-rise buildings, several of them more than twenty storeys high.

FEE HOUSE

The Thomas Fee House at **1401 Pendrell Street** is a mish-mash of Queen Anne flair and Edwardian touches. The purple bell tower built over stone is an eye-stopper. Now painted light green with yellow trim and sitting between modern high-rises, the house looks like it stepped out of the pages of a bizarre fairy tale. Fee, the flamboyant partner of J.E.

Parr in the architectural firm Parr & Fee, designed this home for himself in 1904 at its original address at 1119 Broughton Street. He only briefly lived in the house, and it was probably a practice design for a more elaborate and long gone house at Gilford and Comox. In 1907 the house sold to a Dr. Henry B. Ford. It changed hands again around 1915 when Andrew Allison Logan moved in. Logan was a timber broker and brother of Matthew Logan of Kitsilano. Logan lived in the Broughton Street house until his death in 1930. The house then sold to James Collins, a waiter at the Georgia Hotel, and his wife Mary. As with most of the grand mansions that remained, the Collins ran it as a boarding house. In 1994, the house went through a total renovation and condo conversion.

BUCHAN HOUSE

Ewing Buchan must have spent many a night after trudging home from a hard day at the bank jotting down the English lyrics to Canada's national anthem. Who would have thought it would stick, at least for a decade or two? The song was a favourite in the West End house, and daughter Olive would belt out the tune on the piano. The lyrics were performed at the Vancouver Club in February 1910, and as a plaque in front of the house at **1114 Barclay Street** proudly acknowledges, *"Built 1897 here in this house 'O Canada' Buchan version was written in 1909."* Unfortunately not everyone shared Buchan's enthusiasm for the song. It lost out around 1929 to the version by R.S. Weir that every school kid sings today. By 1915, the Buchans moved to Shaughnessy, and Dr. Robert F. Greer was living in the O Canada House.

The modest Queen Anne O Canada House is one of only two houses left on the street, the rest of the block contains apartment buildings. The apartment building at **1170 Barclay Street** housed the famous Italian sculptor Charles Marega and his wife Berta in the early 1930s. It's a simple two-storey, grey stucco affair with palm trees carved into the cement above the door, which evidently gave it the improbable name of "The Florida." Like most artists, it seems Marega, who changed his name from Carlos to Charles in the 1920s, couldn't afford expensive digs and didn't become really famous until after his death. While his name is not widely known today, most people know his work. His two lion statues grace the south end of the Lions Gate Bridge. He is the creator of the bronze bust of David Oppenheimer, Vancouver's second mayor, which sits at the entrance to Stanley Park, as well as a fountain honouring King Edward VII near the Vancouver Art Gallery. His fourteen famous people statues adorn the Francis Rattenbury Parliament

Buildings in Victoria, and the statue of Captain Vancouver in front of Vancouver City Hall is a Marega. Marega also sculpted the controversial maidens for L.D. Taylor that hold up what was once the World Tower (now the Sun Tower) on Beatty Street. Trained in plaster, his ceilings were in demand by the wealthy before the First World War. Marega taught at the Vancouver School of Decorative and Applied Arts—today more familiar as the Emily Carr Institute of Art & Design. At sixty-eight-years-old, just as he started to finally receive recognition for his famous sculpture of the lions in Stanley Park, a heart attack struck. He had just finished teaching a class when he keeled over dead. Marego's work also adorns Alvo von Alvensleben's mansion (now Crofton House School), Harry Reifel's Rio Vista, Hycroft in Shaughnessy Heights, and Shannon at Fifty-seventh Avenue and Granville.

By 1914 the West End was no longer as much fun for the rich. The middle class (riff raff to the rich) had moved in, industry was creeping closer, and apartment buildings were obstructing the view. Fortunately for the elite, by the second decade of the century, Shaughnessy Heights was well underway and most fled to the curving boulevards and huge properties to build their new mansions, leaving their cast offs to become apartments and rooming houses.

WEST END PLANE CRASH

British Columbia Lumberman, September 1918: "It is a matter of poignant regret that the forest scouting hydro-aeroplane built to the order of the B.C. Government by Hoffars Bros of Vancouver has had its career cut short at the very outset. The accident was due to the engine missing fire. The plucky aviator, Lieut. V.A. Bishop, is to be congratulated on what was a miraculous escape from instant death."

A 1918 newspaper published what must have been that year's best picture. It shows a seaplane sticking out of the roof of one of the larger West End houses. A close look reveals the pilot peering out of a hole in the roof big enough to drive a Hummer through. The department of forestry ordered one of these new-fangled flying machines to patrol large tracts of land in the province. Victor Bishop, a twenty-three-year-old pilot, was on a three-month furlough from the Royal Naval Air Force in England visiting his aunt who happened to live two blocks away from the crash site. While in Vancouver, he took the plane for his second test flight. To the fascination of thousands of craned necks, Bishop flew over the Burrard Inlet and over the city, circling out over False Creek, and then sud-

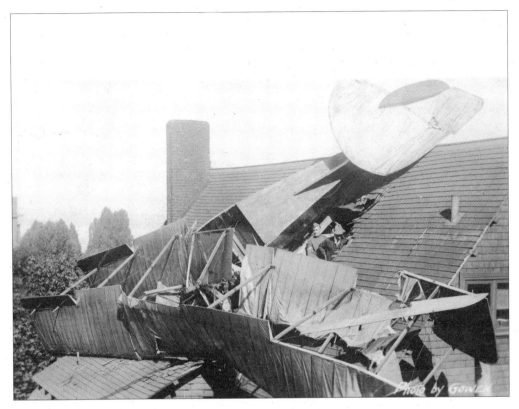

SEAPLANE CRASHING THROUGH WEST END ROOF, SEPTEMBER 4, 1918.
CITY OF VANCOUVER ARCHIVES. PHOTO #AIR P31
PHOTOGRAPHER: FRANK GOWEN

denly dropped twelve thousand feet and crashed into the roof of Dr. James Farish, a Vancouver ear, eye, and nose specialist.

Jimmy and Henry Hoffar, the brothers who built the seaplane, were watching the test flight from a boat near their Coal Harbour shop and waiting for its return. "They rushed to the place where Bishop fell and took charge of the wreckage. Policemen and firemen came to the Farish home and but for the good work of these officials the immense crowd which gathered would probably have wrecked the entire house in their stampede for souvenirs."

"The wings were spread out upon the roof so that an excellent view was afforded to the crowds below," wrote a reporter. "Lt. Bishop apparently lost considerable blood as a result of his injuries, for the gore mixed with the gasoline from the engine and dripped down the side of the building."

Dr. Farish, who was out at the time, came home to find a very banged up Bishop walking out his front door at 755 Bute Street. Farish, more concerned with the health of the pilot than the shape of his roof, rode with him to the hospital. Bishop was treated with applications of cracked ice.

Chapter 6

SHAUGHNESSY HEIGHTS: HAVEN FOR THE RICH

Credit the Canadian Pacific Railway for much of the development of early Vancouver, but the CPR was just in practice mode before 1909. By that year, the CPR had real-estate development down to a fine art and was ready to unveil the piece de resistance: Shaughnessy Heights above the hilly slopes south of False Creek.

Around the turn of the century, this parcel of about two hundred and fifty acres of brush and stumps far from the downtown core had amazing money-making potential for the CPR. And, just as the condo marketers of this century hype up new projects with glossy sales pitches, the CPR designed and positioned Shaughnessy for the rich. And the rich bought. They fled their West End mansions for the curvy tree-lined boulevards, broad lawns, and promised golf courses, tennis courts, and lawn bowls of Shaughnessy Heights.

In the summer of 1909, an army of twelve hundred workers cut roads, built sidewalks, and laid sewer lines. And when the first lots went on sale a year later, hundreds of Vancouver's wealthier citizens lined up along Hastings Street for the chance to buy in. By 1914 there were two hundred and forty three households living behind hedgerows in Shaughnessy Heights, eighty percent of which had a listing in the Vancouver Social Register. Architecture ranged from Georgian Revival manors to Spanish Colonial Haciendas, and from Cape Cod cottages to oversized Californian bungalows on lots that varied in size from one-fifth of an acre to one and a half acres. Prospective buyers had to agree to spend at least six thousand dollars on a house, about six times that of the going rate, and the CPR offered financing at a six percent interest rate to sweeten the deal. Presumably to assist in keeping the neighbourhood both exclusive and white, many of the CPR deeds of sale included their own single family clauses as well as restrictive covenants forbidding the resale of property to "Orientals."

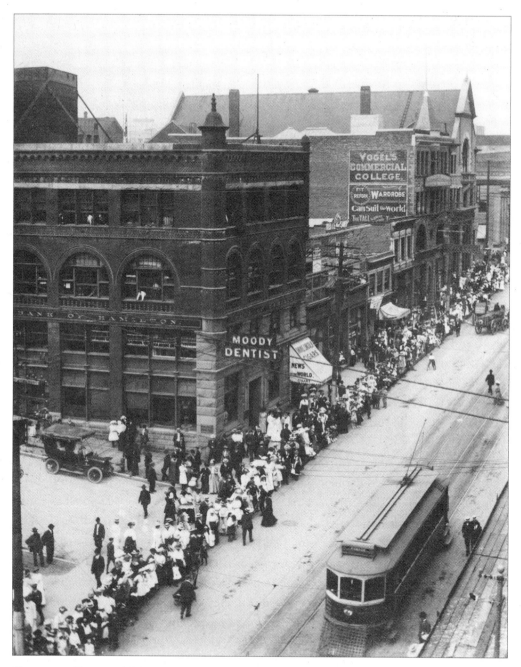

Hundreds of Vancouver's Wealthiest Citizens Line Up to Buy a Lot in Shaughnessy Heights.
City of Vancouver Archives. Photo #CVA 677-653. Circa 1909.
Photographer: Philip T. Timms

In those hallowed carefree early days of Shaughnessy heights, before the Janet Smith murder, before the Ku Klux Klan moved their headquarters into Matthews Avenue, before the Wall Street Crash of 1929, and before the area got the nicknames of "Poverty Hill" and "Mortgage Heights," Shaughnessy folk lived a happy social existence of parties, rides in polished Cadillacs and Packards, and long afternoons sipping lemonade by the swimming pool.

ARDVAR

In 1907, Richard Marpole, who had taken over from Harry Abbott as general superintendent of the CPR, announced the company's plans to create a two million dollar exclusive enclave for Vancouver's upper class. Marpole owned Ardvar: the first house built in Shaughnessy Heights on a huge block at **1675 Marpole Street** at the corner of Angus Drive. Marpole Street and the district of Marpole are namesakes of Richard Marpole, who was a CPR manager when the first passenger trains crossed Canada. After Marpole died in 1920, the three-storey house sold to John W. Stewart, a partner in Foley, Welch and Stewart, a huge railway contracting firm that built much of the Grand Trunk Pacific Line, parts of Pacific Great Eastern and the CNR. Stewart lived there until his death in 1938.

THOMAS SHAUGHNESSY HOUSE

The neighbourhood and its streets, named in honour of Sir Thomas George Shaughnessy, president of the CPR from 1898 to 1918, reads like a modern-day street directory. The lyrical sounding Marguerite Street gets its name from Shaughnessy's daughter. Other CPR directors, such as Richard Bladforth Angus, Richard Marpole, Sir Edmund Osler, W.D. Matthews, C.R. Hosmer, and Sir Augustus Nanton, also lent their last names to streets in the district.

One of the next houses built after Marpole's was for Shaughnessy himself, at **1551 Angus Drive.** The story goes that Shaughnessy, an American railroader, got his job as general purchasing agent for the CPR over a glass of Milwaukee beer. Knighted in 1901, he became Lord Shaughnessy in 1916, seven years before he died at age seventy. The ten thousand square foot house was supposed to replicate an Irish hunting lodge, but wound up looking more like an English Arts and Craft. Shaughnessy spent most of his time in Montreal, and the mansion was little more than a summer house for his family. But being an influential kind of a guy, having him as a neighbour inspired others to follow. Between 1908 and 1914 there were well over two hundred mansions in Shaughnessy Heights, and by the time Shaughnessy sold his house in 1917 to Costello Weston Frazee, supervisor at the Royal Bank, the area was the newest enclave for the rich. The Frazee family owned the house until 1954. In 2006 the house rated the number eighteen spot as most expensive in the city, assessed at close to eight million dollars. Not bad for a weekend getaway.

W. F. SALSBURY HOUSE

Another early Shaughnessy resident, William Ferriman Salsbury, spent twenty five thousand dollars on his three-storey house at **1790 Angus Drive** in 1912. Salsbury's house had a conservatory, a huge billiard room, and tennis courts. Salsbury, another CPR executive, arrived in British Columbia on the first transcontinental train and moved from his digs in the West End to join his contemporaries in Shaughnessy Heights. After Salsbury retired to Victoria in 1921, he sold the house to Edward A. Morris, a successful Vancouver tobacconist.

The same year Salsbury moved to Victoria, his son Bill Salsbury junior was shot to death at close range while walking down Georgia Street just near Burrard Street in downtown Vancouver. The fact that it was only 8:00 P.M., that he was a well-liked forty-three-year-old accountant, together with the senselessness of his murder, shocked the city. Police figured that instead of handing over cash, Salsbury had tried to fight off robbers with his umbrella, which they later found badly bent. A Vancouver native, the newspaper described him as one of the best known residents of Vancouver, an excellent horseman, and a sportsman who belonged to both the rowing club and the Royal Vancouver Yacht Club. It was a tough case for police. The only clue they had was a small piece of material they'd found caught on a barbed wire fence the killers had climbed when they fled. Weeks went by, the Salsbury family hired a private detective, but still no leads turned up. Then police caught a break with the report of a theft of clothes from a downtown rooming house. Police rounded up a suspect, found a pawn ticket in his pocket, and retrieved the stolen clothes. Remarkably, they saw that a pair of pants had a piece torn from the leg that matched the material from the barbed wire fence. The thief told them that he'd received the stolen clothes from Alexander "Frenchie" Paulson who had bragged about the murder to him and had mentioned that he had torn his pants while running away with his buddy Allan

Robinson. Paulson confessed, and police found Robinson in Oakalla Prison, serving a four-month sentence for vagrancy. The trial went ahead six months later and Paulson and Robinson were hanged. Robinson apparently told witnesses that crime didn't pay.

The June 20, 1936 *Province* has a picture of the senior Salsbury at his Gordon Head Estate, aged ninety, tending to his roses. He is the name behind Salsbury Street in the less-moneyed Grandview Woodlands area. He died in 1938.

THE HOLLIES

Of all the ritzy streets in Shaughnessy Heights, one of the finest is The Crescent. It wraps itself around stately Shaughnessy Park, sits on the highest ground in the area, and is the feeder for other up-market streets such as Angus, McRae, Osler, Hudson, and Tecumseh. The 1915 city directories lists no crass street numbers for these mansions, only names, and THE in The Crescent is typed all in upper case, lest it be mistaken for a less significant address.

Down the curvy road a way is The Hollies at **1388 The Crescent.** Owned originally by George E. MacDonald, general manager of the Pacific Great Eastern Railway, the mansion went up in 1912. The heritage inventory describes the house as a "rambling Neoclassical Revival structure." With its giant entrance and huge columns, it looks like it would be at home on some exclusive Greek island. It's deceptive from the front gate, but inside, the mansion has six bedrooms, a retractable roof, five fireplaces, an indoor pool, a putting green, tennis courts, a playground, and a coach house. MacDonald sold the house with its two acres of land in 1921 to Alexander Robert Mann, president of Northern Construction Ltd. A former CPR executive, Mann started up his own road-building firm in 1904. His first contract was the James Bay Road from Toronto to Sudbury. He married Jennie in 1907, and they moved to Vancouver five years later. The Manns lived at the Hollies until the early 1940s when Sir Walter Carpenter and his wife Edith moved in. The city directories list Carpenter as president of W.R. Carpenter Canada, a manufacturer of coconut, linseed, and other vegetable oils and oil cake. The Hollies changed hands a couple of times after that, and in 1950 became a guest house, at one point apparently paying its property taxes as a wedding reception hall.

A *Vancouver Sun* story of May 1991 reports that Norman Keevil, the late mining executive, paid just under three million dollars for the thirteen thousand square foot house in 1983. During the 1980s he did extensive renovations, including an Arthur Erickson designed indoor pool with a retractable roof and new patios, and a tennis court on three acres. Ironically, considering the exclusion of "Orientals" in the first stage of Shaughnessy's development, in 1991 the address changed from 1350 to 1388 The Crescent to attract Asian buyers. The number eight, especially a pair of eights, symbolizes prosperity to the Chinese, but it apparently wasn't enough to make up for the hefty price tag and property taxes because no one came forward to buy it. In 1996 The Hollies was up for sale again, this time for fifteen million dollars. Four years after it was first listed, the mansion sold for six-and-a-half million dollars. Assessed at just under ten million dollars, in 2006 The Hollies was the ninth most valuable house in Vancouver.

THE VILLA RUSSE

A later entrant to The Crescent is Misak Yremavitch Aivazoff, a local money man and arts lover, and his wife Aileen. Aivazoff moved into The Villa Russe at **3390 The Crescent** in 1922, a white Tuscan style house called a Second Renaissance Revival Façade. Aivazoff lived the good life. He loved to entertain and counted visiting Russian nobility among his frequent guests. More famous guests of the time included Grant Duke Alexander, Serge Rachmanioff, and Prince Obelinsky. Unfortunately Aivazoff, who is listed in the city directories as president of New Method Coal and Supplies, did not do well in the Depression, and the house changed hands to H.A. Wallace, the shipbuilder in the early 1930s.

Directory entries suggest that Aivazoff never regained a financial foothold in the city. He and his wife Aileen bumped around to a few different Shaughnessy addresses, likely short-term rentals, during the '30s. In 1938, Aileen lived at 856 Howe Street and was the proprietor of the Hampton House, which was at one point an antique dealer and at another, an apartment building. By 1953 Misak had moved to a Jervis Street address in the West End and died the following year, aged seventy-eight.

In 1946, B.C. Electric bought The Villa Russe from Wallace, and Albert Edward (Dal) Grauer, head of the company, and his family moved in. Sherry Grauer was eight when she and three siblings moved into the house, which she describes as Mediterranean. Sherry Grauer, a renowned artist now living on Vancouver Island, says, surprisingly the house only had three bedrooms, so her father built an addition on the back and a pool with a cabana designed by family friend Arthur Erickson. By the 1940s, many of these huge rambling houses were becoming apartments, and Sherry's grandmother, Zipporam Woodward, lived in one a few doors down.

THE GRAUER CHILDREN IN FRONT OF VILLA RUSSE, 1958.
PHOTO COURTESY OF CHRISTOPHER GRAUER.

Sherry's mother painted portraits and flowers, and Sherry remembers going upstairs to bed while her father played Chopin or Schubert on the piano. "Music was a very important thing in his life," she says. "He was an audiophile, always trying to get the very best LP equipment, and he'd lie on the sofa and listen."

By 1961, Dal Grauer, dying with leukemia, continued to battle the B.C. Government over its decision to take over the company (now B.C. Hydro). The government announced the takeover the day of Grauer's funeral. Still, he managed to kick back from the grave. Sherry says her father incorporated his two-million-dollar-plus estate into a family company in another province and legally stiffed the government for estate taxes. "And that made Wacky Bennett very cross," says his daughter. He left his stamp on the B.C. Electric Building (now the Elektra), built in 1957, and the Dal Grauer Substation. One of Sherry's early memories was wandering over to Shaughnessy Park across the road to put on plays for the veterans who lived at Hycroft after the McRaes left the mansion.

HYCROFT

For a few years, at least, General Alexander Duncan McRae had an avenue named after him as well as the only manor on it. And what a place it is. Hycroft took three years to build, and by 1911 the thirty-room mansion was the best in the area. McRae paid around ten thousand dollars for five-and-a-half acres and another hundred thousand dollars for the mansion, at **1489 McRae Avenue**, at a time when thirty five hundred dollars bought you fancy digs. One of the city's earliest multimillionaires, McRae was also a senator, and a society figure who successfully dabbled in lumber, fish, coal, and real estate.

Hycroft sits on the brow of the hill with a view of Vancouver and in its heyday, had a formal drawing room, conservatory, billiard room, library, two dining rooms, a full-sized lounge, a bar, and a wine cellar that held two thousand bottles. Another building housed the indoor swimming pool, squash courts, and a bowling alley, while outside were badminton and tennis courts, and an Italian garden landscaped with terraces and lawns and planted only with blue and yellow flowers—Blaunche McRae's favourite colours. It took a staff of ten, a cook, and master gardener to keep the house going day to day. The servants (none of them Chinese—McRae was a member of the Asiatic Exclusion League) went about their work in hidden passageways.

The annual masked ball at Hycroft on New Year's Eve was the height of the social set for the Shaughnessy crowd. It was held in the downstairs ballroom on floorboards packed with dried seaweed to give extra bounce.

When McRae moved into Hycroft, the land was treeless. There's a story that has him spotting a rare sequoia tree in New Westminster, originally purchased in California. After hearing that the tree wouldn't survive a second transplant, much less a fifteen mile journey, McRae had a special wagon made, and had the tree carted by a ten-horse team all the way along a logging road to Shaughnessy. The sequoia is now about one hundred feet high and thriving. A copper beech tree that he had planted is purported to be the largest in Western Canada.

By the time World War Two rolled around, the McRaes, fed up with sky-high heating bills and a shortage of servants, sold the mansion in 1942 to the government for one dollar. Not knowing the meaning of downsize, McRae retired to a massive log house designed by Vancouver architect C.B.K. Van Norman, called Eaglecrest, his thirty-seven hundred acre property in Qualicum Beach. For two years at the height of the Depression, McRae employed twenty-five men full time on the construction of the house, which, when finished, was made of whole cedar logs and included lawn bowling, and golf putting greens.

Blaunche McRae died in 1942, and McRae, who married again the following year, died in 1946. That year *The Vancouver Sun* speculated that Bing Crosby would fork over $320,000 for the house and its 320 acres, but the entire spread, including Dorset horn sheep, Lincolnshire cattle, and Yorkshire pigs, sold to Leonard Boultbee, president of Boultbee & Sweet. Boultbee was a prosperous realtor who, with his wife Helen, had recently bought 1675 Angus Drive—the first house built in Shaughnessy Heights for Richard Marpole. Boultbee flipped much of the Qualicum Beach property and surrounding woodlands to H.R. MacMillan, the lumber tycoon, the following year. In June 1948, he opened Eaglecrest as an exclusive resort that could accommodate twenty-two well-heeled guests.

Hycroft served as a hospital between 1943 and 1960. It then sat empty for two years until the University Women's Club bought it in 1962. In those days women were not allowed to hold mortgages, and the club paid in full. The club members raised the cash in a year, but it took another five to evict the raccoons, cut out the blackberry vines, and clean up the interior.

W.C. Nichol House

McRae wasn't alone on his street for long. In 1913 Walter Cameron Nichol, owner of *The Province* newspaper, built a combination of Tudor Revival and English Arts and Crafts at **1402 McRae Avenue**. Designed by Maclure and Fox, the massive ten thousand square foot house with its tall chimneys, leaded glass windows and eight fireplaces, stretched across three large lots. Nichol, who incidentally is the only journalist to make lieutenant-governor, held the job from 1920 to 1926. He moved to Sidney in 1925 to another mansion called Miraloma, also designed by Samuel Maclure. From 1925, mining engineer W.R. Wilson lived at the McRae Street manor until Leopold and Antoinette Bentley and their son Peter took it over in 1940.

The Bentleys are known today as the founders of Canfor, the world's largest exporter of softwood lumber; but in 1938, they had just barely escaped Vienna on Anschluss: the date Austria was taken over by the Nazis. Leopold Bloch-Bauer, a Jewish industrialist, his wife Antoinette, a world class equestrian, and their young son Peter fled to Switzerland. The Gestapo arrested Leopold but later released him, and he escaped Austria to reunite with his family and then fled to Canada. When they applied for Canadian citizenship in 1938, they changed their last name to Bentley. Antoinette's brother John Pick also immigrated to Canada, changing his name to Prentice. Bentley and Prentice started Pacific Veneer in 1938 and changed the name to Canadian Forest Products. Leopold died in 1986, but his family kept his house at 1402 McRae until Antoinette died in 2004. The house sold in 2005 for seven million dollars.

M.P. COTTON HOUSE

As the company prospered, Leopold's brother-in-law and partner John Prentice initial-ly rented rooms in, and then, in 1939, bought **1537 Matthews Avenue**. Miles P. Cotton had the Colonial-Revival house built in 1913. The owner of Cotton & Co., the firm that cleared and developed Shaughnessy Heights for the CPR, Cotton quarried much of the stone that built the Shaughnessy roads and sidewalks from the South Vancouver rock pit, now the Quarry Gardens in Queen Elizabeth Park on Little Mountain.

The Matthews Avenue house is a magnificent stone mansion with lots of stained glass, a large hedge, and a massive monkey tree in the front yard. The architect is unknown, but the house is similar to two of Samuel Maclure's Victoria houses. The main floor was con-structed using a variety of different rocks. Most would have come from the quarry, but others are likely to be from rubble blasted out of The Rockies by the CPR.

During the 1950s, Prentice added a basement and finished the rec room in a rather startling assortment of Canfor products. In 1963, Arthur Erickson designed an addition that included an indoor swimming pool.

Incidentally, in 1918, Cotton's neighbour across the road at the much more modest **1538 Matthews Avenue** was Ewing Buchan, the liquidator at the Bank of Vancouver fresh from the West End and the writer of an "O Canada" version.

GLEN BRAE

A block away, Glen Brae mansion had a fascinating history before it became Canuck Place children's hospice in the early 1990s. Designed by Parr and Fee in 1911 for William Lamont Tait, a retired lumber and real estate tycoon, the Queen Anne mansion at **1690 Matthews Avenue** takes its name from Tait's Scottish homeland and means "valley of the mountains." It is personal taste as to whether it's hideous or beautiful, but apparently it reminded Tait of castles back home. The ornate wrought iron fence out front was an

GLEN BRAE, 1690 MATTHEWS, NOVEMBER, 1925.
CITY OF VANCOUVER ARCHIVES. PHOTO # CVA 99-1494.
PHOTOGRAPHER: STUART THOMSON.

import from Scotland and cost ten thousand dollars, more than the cost of the average manor in those days. The mansion has eighteen rooms and six tiled bathrooms. One of the bathrooms has a huge stained glass window of a sailing scene, and over the oak staircase, another depicting a small cottage in the Scottish highlands. Glen Brae had one of the first elevators in the province and a ballroom big enough to handle two hundred and fifty dancers covered the entire third floor. Tait died in 1919 and his wife a year later, after which the house went into a slow decline.

In 1925, Glen Brae became the headquarters of the Kanadian Knights of the Ku Klux Klan, and gained some notoriety. The Klan has a listing in the city directories for that year. While the gentry didn't want to live next door to the not-so-white, they were nonetheless uncomfortable with the parades of folk in white robes and hoods carrying lit-up crosses through the tree lined streets of Shaughnessy.

Chuck Davis writes on vancouverhistory.ca that the KKK membership in Vancouver was supposed to be eight thousand at its peak. "This is likely an exaggeration. At any rate, a local bylaw was passed prohibiting mask-wearing and the number of Klan members

GLEN BRAE, 1690 MATTHEWS, ONE-TIME HEADQUARTERS OF THE KKK. NOVEMBER, 1925.
CITY OF VANCOUVER ARCHIVES. PHOTO #CVA 99-1496.
PHOTOGRAPHER: STUART THOMSON.

dwindled to about 200. The sheeted twits were out of Glen Brae in less than a year, even though their rent was only $150 a month." Davis adds that he still has an old newspaper ad showing Glen Brae as a prize in a raffle with tickets at one dollar each.

A few years after the Klan left, the sixteen thousand square foot mansion briefly housed Glen Brae Academy, a primary school. By the 1930s the locals started calling Glen Brae the Mae West because its double domed design resembled certain physical attributes of the sexy film queen.

Although appraisers had valued the mansion at $75,000 in the 1920s, by 1939, Glen Brae sold for only $7,500 to Francis Wright and his wife Stella. That year, the city directory lists Wright as secretary treasurer for something called S.D. & W. After the Wrights left in the mid-'50s, Glen Brae became a rest home for a while, and then by 1980, it had turned into a private hospital occupied by a number of elderly women. The elevator became a dumbwaiter used to bring the ladies food from the kitchen. Julian and Elisabeth Wlosinksi who lived upstairs turned the fifteen-metre long ballroom into a living room flanked by two bedrooms, each of which boasted ten arched windows. Elisabeth Wlosinksi donated the mansion to the city in 1991.

JOHN HENDRY HOUSE

Like William Lamont Tait, John Hendry was another wealthy lumber man with expensive tastes. The John Hendry House at **3802 Angus Drive** and Matthews Avenue, was actually built in 1913 by architects to the rich, Samuel Maclure and Cecil Fox, for J.E. Tucker, president of the Vancouver Lumber Company. Although Tucker was a Texan, his Tudor Revival style house fit the British character of the fledging neighbourhood. But whether Tucker had built the house as a speculative venture, or simply became tired of Shaughnessy, by the following year, he was building an Arts and Crafts style mansion on millionaire's row on South West Marine Drive. Tucker sold the Angus Drive house to Hendry, the owner of B.C. Mills, Timber and Trading.

Another refugee from the West End, Hendry lived at 1281 Burnaby Street, his house long ago demolished to make way for a huge concrete apartment tower, with "The Hendry House" painted on the front door. Hendry died in 1916 and only lived at the Angus Drive address for a year. But because he was the most prominent resident, his name sticks to the mansion. A one-time mayor of New Westminster, Hendry bought the first gasoline-powered car in 1905.

Hendry hired Harry Hooper as the city's first chauffeur. Hooper was a bit of an eccentric and had made a name for himself as the 1903 half-mile bicycle champion of B.C. He incorporated Vancouver's first taxi cab company in 1937. Hooper told Vancouver archivist Major Matthews that Hendry paid over a thousand dollars for the car. "I knew it very well, because I drove it," he told Major Matthews, adding, "I learned to drive in 1904 in a two-cylinder Ford. It took about two hours, figuratively speaking, to go around [Stanley] Park." Hooper added that Hendry's car was a single-cylinder, one-lung Oldsmobile.

Hendry once owned the Hastings Sawmill and the land that is now John Hendry Park, which his daughter Aldyen donated to the city. Hendry's name lives on in Hendry Avenue in North Vancouver and Hendry Place in New Westminster. After his death, his wife Adaline hung on to the mansion until the early 1930s where it languished for another decade until Willis P. Dewees, the former general manager at the Strand Theatre, moved in.

GREENCROFT

Aldyen Hendry found another mover and shaker in Eric Hamber, a Canadian banker working in London. Born in Winnipeg, Hamber attended St. John's College, where his dad was the headmaster, and excelled in sports—rugby, football, hockey, tennis, rowing— and captained a Winnipeg team in the Stanley Cup. Eric and Aldyen planned to marry in London in 1912, thwarting John Hendry's gift of a passage home on the newly minted Titanic. The following year, the Hambers moved back to Vancouver and took up residence at **3838 Cypress Street,** a twelve thousand square foot mansion they named the English sounding "Greencroft," complete with a large chateau style tower, wooden colonnade, and conservatory.

Hamber left the staid world of banking for the lucrative world of wood, working with his father-in-law at B.C. Mills. Outside of work, Hamber loved his thoroughbreds, and in the hungry '30s bought a thousand-acre stock farm in Coquitlam called Minnekhada, a Sioux word meaning beside still waters. He built a country retreat and Scottish hunting lodge in the Tudor Revival style and brought his buddies up from the city to play polo and hunt pheasants and ducks.

Hamber was lieutenant-governor from 1936 to 1940, and guests that stayed at Greencroft and Minnekhada included Franklin Roosevelt and Louis St. Laurent. The lodge still has a room called the "Royal Suite," named after King George VI. Queen Elizabeth II also stopped in for a visit during her Dominion tour in 1939. In 1958 the Hambers sold the Minnekhada Ranch to another past lieutenant-governor and Shaughnessy neighbour, Clarence Wallace, president of Burrard Dry Dock Company. Wallace kept the royal suite in use with visitors that included Prince Axel of Denmark and Prince Bernhardt of the Netherlands. Since 1981, the lodge and the farm has been the property of the Greater Vancouver Regional District.

The Hambers kept Greencroft until Eric's death in 1960. In 2006, Greencroft was listed as the twelfth most expensive house at an annual assessment of just under nine million dollars. It sits on nearly a full acre of land with one hundred-year-old maple trees, two detached guest houses, and close to scads of old money. The name lives on at Hamber Island, in Indian Arm, once owned by the family, Hamber Provincial Park on the B.C./Alberta border, and the Eric Hamber Secondary School in Vancouver. Aldyen lived until one hundred and three. The Special Collections room at the Vancouver Public Library is named after her.

ROSEMARY

Rosemary, a Tudor Revival style mansion at **3689 Selkirk Street**, is another house built by Samuel Maclure and his partner Cecil Fox. They finished it in 1915. The house first belonged to lawyer and liquor tycoon Albert Edward Tulk who named the house after his only daughter, and lived there until 1924. In 1928, J.W. Fordham Johnson, B.T. Rogers' successor at the B.C. Sugar Company, moved here from his home at 1389 The Crescent.

Named lieutenant-governor of B.C. in 1931, Johnson presumably moved to Carey Castle in Victoria, and likely rented Rosemary to the next resident wealthy financier, Austin Cottrel Taylor. Taylor owned the Bralorne Gold Mine and liked to race horses, which trained at his A.C.T. stock farm in Langley. Why monogram a shirt when you can initial an entire farm? His horse Indian Broom placed third in the Kentucky Derby and brought home three thousand dollars. During World War Two, Taylor worked for the war minister C.D. Howe for one dollar a year. He also chaired the B.C. Security Commission, which interned the Japanese. Taylor's daughter Patricia married American conservative William. F. Buckley.

After Johnson retired in 1936, Eric Hamber became lieutenant-governor. Taylor bought Shannon at Fifty-seventh Avenue and Granville from Mary Rogers, and Johnson moved back to the hallowed halls of Rosemary. Johnson died in 1938, and his wife lived at Rosemary until 1942. By 1949, Rosemary became a retreat house for the Convent of Our Lady of the Cenacle. In the 1990s, new owners subdivided the property and built two large houses on the land. Unable to be torn down because of its heritage value, and too expensive to renovate, it's now used mainly as the backdrop for spooky movies and television series. The grand entrance makes a great space for a hotel desk and the rest room by the front door boasts dozens, maybe hundreds, of handpainted blue and white tiles. Every tile is different, and the scenes vary from windmills, to fisherman, to small children.

Rosemary on Selkirk, the John Hendry House on Angus Drive, and Walter Nichol House on McRae, were all the work of architect Samuel Maclure while he lived in Victoria.

Partnered first with Cecil Fox and later with Ross Lort, he made his reputation building these massive Tudor Revival houses, but Maclure's versatility is most evident in his earliest work in New Westminster.

Chapter 7

As an architect, Samuel Maclure was obsessively hands on. After he left New Westminster for Victoria, he would regularly catch the CPR midnight boat from Victoria—an eight hour trip—to supervise the Vancouver work. He never owned a car and would travel to mansions such as Gabriola on Davie Street in the West End, to Brock House on Point Grey Road and the John Hendry house in Shaughnessy Heights by streetcar, often reading the *Oxford Book of Verse*. While most of the mansions, including Aberthau, now the West Point Grey Community Centre on West Second Avenue, still stand, Maclure has his fingerprints all over dozens of houses around British Columbia.

The son of a Royal Engineer, Maclure was born in Sapperton in 1860 and grew up on the family property in Matsqui. His elder sister Sara was the first woman telegrapher in British Columbia, maybe in Canada. She later married John McLagan, owner of the *Vancouver Daily World*, which she continued to run for a while after he died, eventually selling out to Vancouver's serial mayor L.D. Taylor. Young Sam followed his sister's example and worked as a telegrapher in Vancouver before spending a year at an art school in Philadelphia and turning to architecture.

Before he moved to Victoria in 1891, Maclure made his architectural mark in New Westminster. He had considerable design range. The small cottage at **375 Keary Street** in Sapperton is one of five small rental houses once owned by future mayor William Keary, and built for workers at the Royal Columbian Hospital and the Brunette Sawmill. At the other end of the spectrum is the flamboyant Charles Murray house, later called Rostrevor, built for five thousand dollars in 1890.

ROSTREVOR

Maclure and his partner Charles Clow designed the Victorian Queen Anne mansion at **403 St. George Street** and Fourth Avenue. A decorator and an artist, Charles Murray wanted the house as a show piece for his work. An imported mantel adorns the fireplace. Bloomfield and Sons, at the time residents and business owners of New Westminster, created the art glass, and Murray himself created the wall frescoes using unique local wood. Murray didn't keep the mansion long as business declined during the 1890s, and the Depression forced him to sell a few years later to Captain James Clarke. In 1901, the house changed hands again when Walter R. Gilley moved in and named it Rostrevor after the family home in Ireland. Gilley, originally from New Brunswick, saw the house through a major renovation around 1916 and transformed it into a mix of original Queen Anne and renovated arts and crafts. The logging company that he ran with brothers James and Herbert was the city's largest contracting supply firm. The Gilleys owned the house until 1961 when it turned into a ritzy boarding house. Apparently, the massive monkey tree in the front lawn was a present for Gilley on the arrival of one of the first boats to pass through the Panama Canal in 1914.

J.A. CUNNINGHAM HOUSE

James Alexander Cunningham's House at **307 Fifth Street** is another example of archi-tect Samuel McClure's versatility. Designed in 1891 by Maclure and then partner Richard Sharp, this Queen Anne house is far more conservative than the Murray House. Supposedly Maclure designed the house for $2,500 from an 1881 pattern book by Rossiter and Wright. It was built on what was once known as Pelham Gardens, where cat-tle roamed and fruit grew, which was laid out by Cunningham's father, Thomas, as part of the 1885 Agricultural fair. In fact, fruit from this piece of land won first prize at the Toronto Exhibition of 1889.

Thomas Cunningham emigrated from Ireland in 1859 and opened Cunningham Hardware in 1862. He was a founder of the Provincial Agricultural Fair at Queen's Park in 1867, the forerunner to Vancouver's Pacific National Exhibition. James inherited the family business acumen it seems. He managed Cunningham Hardware for twenty-three years, then took a series of senior jobs first with the Western Steamboat Company and then with the B.C. Refining Company. He was president of the Board of Trade in 1908 and 1909. James married Marion Debeck in 1889 and had three children. Both Thomas and James are the names behind Cunningham Street.

HILLCROFT

While Maclure later designed the John Hendry House in Shaughnessy Heights, another leading New Westminster architect, George William Grant, who came out from Nova Scotia in 1885 to seek work, designed Hendry's New Westminster house. Unlike Maclure, Grant chose to stay in New Westminster, and is behind much of the city's design character.

Not much exists of the original Hendry house at **725 Queens Avenue**. John Hendry, the timber baron bought up an entire city block and around 1885 built "Hillcroft" perched high on the hill above the Fraser River. Already wealthy from investments in lumber and the railway, and friends with the likes of Sir Wilfrid Laurier, Hendry had Grant design the Victorian mansion as a showcase for his mill's products. Apparently the finished house lacked space, as about a year after it was completed, Hendry added a wing with a billiard room and more bedrooms.

Hendry served as Mayor of New Westminster in 1889, but only lasted six months and resigned in the face of conflict of interest allegations. By the turn of the century, he joined other bluebloods in the move to the West End of Vancouver, but held onto the New Westminster property until about 1911, probably the time he was making tracks to Shaughnessy Heights. At that time he sold the New Westminster property to his neighbour Herbert Gilley, another lumber dealer.

Gilley had the property subdivided into thirteen large lots and had architect E.J. Boughen design a new house that combined the wing with the billiard room of Hendry's mansion with his own 1893 house. The different parts were then loaded onto skids and pulled by eight oxen from the top of the property to its current site. There's a bump in the floor where the two houses join. The Gilley family lived in the house for a couple more decades until the 1940s, when it became a seven suite rooming house. Alan Cruickshank took over the property in 1997 after a succession of owners had passed through. What he bought was an overgrown jungle hiding an eight thousand square-foot dilapidated mansion. In one of the bedrooms, Cruickshank peeled away layers of wallpaper and uncovered a message written on the plaster, "Welcome, Annie Gilley," signed by Herbert Gilley's preteen daughter around 1912.

Grant also designed the 1891 Rand House at **303 Queens Avenue,** once described in a newspaper article as a "princely home." A reporter with *The Ledger* toured the home the year it was built and wrote, "With the exception of Dunsmuir Castle, the proud home of the Dunsmuir family at Victoria, there is not a more splendidly appointed home in British Columbia than that of Mr. Arthur Rand."

THE RAND HOUSE

James Galbraith, who was president of his family's mill working business, bought the Rand House and its huge corner lot in 1925 and proceeded to tear it down and build something smaller. The second house still stands and is a rambling place with large bay windows and a stone foundation. A picture of the original Rand House shows a huge Victorian-style mansion with an enormous turret and art glass designed by McCausland and Son of Toronto. "He tore it down to build a modern home for his family," says current owner Marcia Horricks. "He was dead set against living in one of those oppressive old places." Fortunately Galbraith hung onto some of the original lamps and the stained glass windows. City directories list Galbraith living in the house until 1935. He died in 1951 at the age of eighty three and the funeral record lists him as owner of Galbraith Ltd. Sawmill.

Horricks says for many years there was a story that the fireplace came from a Scottish Castle. Unfortunately, she says, it looks like they've debunked that myth. "I think the tiles are from a very famous American fellow who did a lot of fireplaces in California at the time," she says.

The house at 303 Queens Avenue changed hands several times over the next few decades and sold in the mid-'70s to Randy Bachman, the famous rock star of the Guess Who and Bachman Turner Overdrive. In Bachman's biography, he talks about constantly touring while his wife Lorayne and two young children stayed first in a West Vancouver trailer park and then briefly in a rented house in South Surrey on a hill looking back at New Westminster. "Being from Winnipeg, to us this was like a Hollywood view, because in Winnipeg when you looked out your back window all you saw were other houses," he says. Bachman talks about the family driving out to New Westminster. "These houses were incredible. We would drive down Queen's Avenue and ogle the beautiful, spacious houses until one day we spotted a 'For Sale' sign on a corner lot house at 303 Queens Avenue. I had always lived on corner lots with my parents. We bought it for $79,000. It was like the *Leave It To Beaver* dream house, only bigger. It was a great house. It had a cool attic with

The House at 303 Queens Avenue, New Westminster. Replaced the Original Rand Mansion in 1925. Photo Courtesy of Marcia Horricks.

all these gables and a large basement. We later renovated the attic to put rooms in it and the basement became my studio." The Bachmans lived in the house for less than two years and took the art glass windows to his music studio in Washington State.

Breezehurst

The prolific Grant designed Breezehurst at **122 First Street** for George and Annie Brymner. Brymner, fresh from Montreal, opened the first West Coast branch of the Bank of Montreal and as manager, no doubt rated a prestigious address to live in. Breezehurst is a large Queen Anne house that sits at the corner of Park Row with a stellar view from its second-floor turret and balcony that's angled to look out over the Fraser River and Queens Park. There, he entertained such visitors as Lady Aberdeen, wife of Canada's Governor General, who in 1895 dropped by for tea in the drawing room. In 1902, Douglas Brymner, George's father and the dominion archivist in Ottawa, died at the house while out on a visit. A north wing, added later, included a billiard room and a master bedroom suite. A conservatory to the south overlooked the tennis court. After Brymner retired,

Breezehurst was home to a succession of Bank of Montreal managers. When the house sold in the 1950s a hideous conversion turned it into an eleven-suite rooming house, and a small apartment block was built on the tennis court. Fortunately the imposing wrought iron fence built by Westminster Ironworks remained, and the house has since reverted to its former single family glory.

For many years, the Brymner's neighbours at the rambling old house at **114 First Street** were the two sisters Mabel and Beatrice with the delightful last name of Cave-Browne-Cave. In *Royal City: The Heritage of New Westminster*, author Jack Scott writes that the Brymner's garden was a favourite meeting place for New Westminster society on weekends. "According to Beatrice Cave-Brown-Cave, who lived next door, on the rare occasions when no other tennis partners could be found, the clerks of the bank were required to participate. It was on the tennis court also that she instructed her first May Day Practices. She learned the May Day dances in Liverpool, England, in 1910 from Cecil Sharp, who had dedicated his life to the revival of folk dancing." Beatrice taught dozens of children original folk dances for the annual May Day festivals.

Beatrice and Mabel moved out from England in 1911 to buy the "Music Connection," a local music school, which they later renamed Stretton Academy after a relative's home in Stretton Abbey, England. Mabel had nineteen letters after her name and played piano, violin, and cello. She taught music full time while Beatrice got a job teaching at John Robson School in New Westminster. After about a year, Beatrice asked that her sixty-five dollars be increased to match Vancouver teachers' salaries of eighty-five dollars a month and was told "certainly not." So she promptly left and taught in Vancouver for the next five years while building up the music school. Mabel died in 1958 and Beatrice lived on until 1987 when she died at Ocean Park in Surrey at one hundred and four.

MR. MAY DAY

Beatrice Cave-Brown-Cave taught the May Day dances, but it was John Joseph Johnston who was Mr. May Day. Johnston was an infant in 1870 when New Westminster crowned its first May Queen, and he attended every May Day after that until his death—aptly on May 1, 1966—at a remarkable ninety-five. He told a reporter that his favourite memory was, "dancing around the maypole in his knickerbockers," and he chaired the May Day committee for nearly half a century.

May Day is still a huge event in the city. According to *The Greater Vancouver Book*, it's the longest running continuing event of its kind in the British Commonwealth, and it is credited for maintaining citizen morale and even ensuring the city's survival.

Johnston's father William and mother Elizabeth were also heavily involved in the community and William ran Johnston Shoes in New Westminster. The store stayed in the family for one hundred and twenty-four years and three generations, selling its last pair of sneakers in December 1983. According to a newspaper article at the time, it was the "rendezvous of businessmen, politicians, and even clergymen who congregated in its back end. Because of this it was known as 'leather parliament'." J.J. probably helped out in the family business and worked for about a decade at the Land Registry Office. It was likely there that he caught the real estate bug, because after working for a while at F.J. Hart & Co. he opened J.J. Johnston Insurance and Real Estate in 1906, the same year he married, and a year later he had Clow and Daniel design his Edwardian house at **125 Third Street**.

Johnston was mayor of New Westminster from 1920 to 1922 and he and his wife Charlotte (Lottie) lived at the Third Street house until the 1950s.

FRED HUME

Fred J. Hume was another popular mayor who served New Westminster in the tough Depression years and through to the start of World War II, between 1933 and 1942. He also had the distinction of serving as Mayor of Vancouver from 1951 to 1958, though his willingness to work for one dollar a year probably helped him get the job. Hume was born in Sapperton in 1892, the grandson of a Royal Engineer, and he spent much of his life in the Moody Park area of New Westminster. As a young man, he played centre for the New Westminster Salmonbellies lacrosse team. The people of New Westminster are a little nutty over lacrosse, maybe because they've always been so good at it. The team started in 1890, playing teams in Vancouver and Victoria. It got the name "Salmonbellies" first as an insult, but held on to it with pride as a reflection of the fishing industry. In 1908, New Westminster won the first Minto Cup as the top pro team in the country and lays claim to being the lacrosse capital of Canada.

In 1924, Hume started CJOR (at that time CFXC) from his basement. He was owner, manager, announcer and disc jockey. The lack of advertising meant no revenue, and he soon sold it to others with a more commercial bent. A listing in the city directories for that time shows him as president of Hume and Rumble, an electrical contracting company, married to Fannie, and living at **1210 Hamilton Street,** a blue two-storey house with a shingle front and leaded windows.

By 1927, business was booming, and the Humes upgraded and moved around the corner to **1001 Edinburgh**, a large white house on a big corner lot with matching garage and gigantic monkey tree in front. Eric Nicol writes in *Vancouver* that he was a "florid, genial person, an immaculate dresser who was naked without the red rose in his buttonhole."

By 1945, Hume had moved again, this time to a large Tudor house at **905 Eighth Avenue**, surrounded by tall cedars and directly opposite Moody Park. Fannie died in 1949, and the following year, city directories show him remarried to Belva and living at **940 Younette Drive** in West Vancouver. In 1961 they moved again, this time to the very upmarket address at **855 Eyremount Drive**, West Vancouver, a sprawling white house on a corner lot with a spectacular view of Vancouver. Hume bought himself a hockey team just after the move, and owned the Vancouver Canucks until his death in 1967. His is the name behind both Hume Street in Queensborough and Hume Park in New Westminster. Hume's annual display of dazzling Christmas lights continues under the current owner Jimmy Pattison. Pattison has added to the tradition and displays a giant star, a two-storey trumpet, and a roof covered in brightly lit stars.

BETH AND JACK WOOD

In the late 1930s, the Woods moved into the tidy green bungalow at **117 St. Patrick Street.** Built in 1925, the home had a variety of owners, including E.R. Beale, a CNR switchman and, during the 30s, Richard James, a local vet, and his wife Jane. The Woods lived in the house until 1964. Jack Wood was a meter man and later superintendent at the Electrical Plant, but his claim to fame was the Gold medal he won as a member of the Canadian Olympic Lacrosse team in 1928. Beth Wood, it seems, was also an overachiever. She was the first woman elected to City Council in 1949 and the first woman to become Mayor of New Westminster. Evidently, she was a popular one, as she held the post from 1959 to 1964. Their tombstones at the Fraser Cemetery in Sapperton read, "Royal City Mayor (Beth) Wood; October 12, 1907 to Sept 18, 1994; founding Governor Simon Fraser University; wife John William Henry (Jack) Wood June 9, 1904 – Sept 10, 1997 A Great Athlete – Olympic Gold Lacrosse Hall of Fame."

Ironically, the cemetery sits on what must be some of the city's best real estate: a hill with sweeping views of the Fraser River and beyond. The twenty-acre cemetery dates back to 1869. It is a fascinating piece of history and a great place for a treasure hunt. Famous New Westminster residents buried there include Raymond Burr, star of "Perry Mason" and "Ironside," who died in 1993. John Deighton, better known as Gassy Jack, the notorious founder of Gastown, didn't have a marked site until the one hundredth anniversary of his death. His marker says, "There Lies John 'Gassy Jack' Deighton (1830-1875) sailor, prospector, steamboat man, pioneer hotel man at New Westminster and Granville, 'I have done well since I came here.'" Steamboat Captain William Irving also lies here, but his best legacy is Irving House, built in 1865 seven years after the founding of New Westminster, and possibly the oldest home in the Lower Mainland.

CAPTAINS

John F. Gosse, another steamboat captain, lived next door to the Wood's house at **119 St. Patrick Street**, in a three-storey Edwardian built in 1908, now painted a radiant yellow. Originally from Newfoundland, Gosse was a mate on the SS Alpha, the first steamer registered in Vancouver. He worked for Union Steamships when they launched the first ferry service to North Vancouver. Gosse died in 1932 at age sixty-seven. He is said to have competed with Captain Wilfred Philpott, another riverboat captain, for most of his career. Paradoxically, years after his death, Philpott's house was saved from demolition and moved from its original spot on Carnarvon Street to St. Patrick Street, right next door to his rival's house.

Philpott's is a Hansel and Gretel looking pink house behind a white picket fence at **121 St. Patrick Street**. Built in 1905, it has a dash of Classical Revival, a dash of Edwardian, and a dash of Arts and Crafts. Philpott named the house "Westham" after a village in Essex England. Philpott, another Maritimer from Port Hawkesbury, Nova Scotia, married Margaret Jane Savage in 1903. He worked as a cook, dredge operator and fireman before rising through the ranks to master mariner. At one point, he ran the Royal City Ice Works from the back of the property, and horses would clop by to pick up ice deliveries. Philpott died in 1945 aged seventy eight. The family hung onto the house until the 70s when it served as a rooming house, later becoming home to a motorcycle gang. It was spruced up after the move to St. Patrick Street in 1990, and in 2002 starred in the Disney film "Ladies and the Champ" with Olympia Dukakis.

While it's not an imposing mansion, the 1911 **Queen's Court Apartments**, designed by

Edwin G.W. Sait, is one of the earliest apartment buildings in the city. Captain Elijah J. Fader originally owned the three-storey cream building at the corner of Second Street and Clinton Place. Fader was born in 1863 in Halifax and came to British Columbia in 1888. He married Lucy Ashby the following year. A story in the New Westminster Museum and Archives says that when Fader was captaining the steamer "Muriel" from Chemainus to Vancouver in 1888, he came across the famous S.S. Beaver wrecked on the rocks below Prospect Point in Stanley Park. "Around midnight he discovered the Beaver in distress on the rocks and went to her assistance. He worked to save her until 4:00 A.M. but after breaking his towline several times gave up as the tide was falling fast and she was expected every moment to sink." Fader ended up saving forty passengers and crew. By 1902, Fader moved to New Westminster and traded the sea for timber, running several companies, including the Vancouver Island Timber syndicate and the B.C. Transportation Company. At one point, he owned more timber land—over 600 square miles—than anyone else in the country. Fader built the Russell Hotel on Carnarvon Street in 1908. From his window in the Queen's Court Apartments, he could easily watch the comings and goings along the river. In 1909, the City of New Westminster named Fader Street in Sapperton after the Captain.

The large Tudor Revival house at **413 Queens Avenue**, built in 1938 for Captain John Sclater, cost the huge sum of nine thousand, five hundred dollars and kept a lot of people employed during the Depression. Born in Scotland in 1894, Sclater came to Canada in 1919. He was the New Westminster harbour master from 1928 until 1959 and started up a private marine survey business after his retirement. Never far from the ocean, he had architect S.W. Hopper include a den in the plans, to be built using cedar beams and oak floors to give the feeling of a ship's cabin. The Dixon's, who bought the house in the mid-1980s, are only the third family to live there. Judy Dixon says they bought the house from Dr. Lawrence and Frances Chipperfield, who had lived there for forty years and raised three children in the home, including Nancy, wife of Premier Gordon Campbell. Dixon says she has the original house plans that show port holes built into either side of the fireplace. "His much younger wife told him that if you put port holes in my Tudor house, I'll have a headache that never goes away. This came from Mrs. Chipperfield," she adds. The rooms all have rounded ceilings and Charles Marega did some of the plaster work, including a lion's head on the fireplace that looks very similar to his more famous ones at the entrance to the Lions Gate Bridge.

QUEENS PARK

From an architectural point of view, New Westminster has everything from Queen Anne mansions to Georgian houses, Tudor Revival, Arts and Crafts and quaint cottages all packed into seven square miles. Unlike other parts of the Lower Mainland where homes predating 1900 are rare, there are dozens of homes dating back to the nineteenth century.

As the waterfront developed and homes started to pop up in downtown New Westminster, the area above Royal Avenue—Queens Park, Uptown, and Brow-of-the-Hill—began to see more growth.

The houses in Queens Park are smaller versions of those in Shaughnessy Heights. Credit for the seventy-five acre Queens Park is due to Peter Latham, a florist and landscape gardener who arrived from Ontario. He was evidently well qualified to design the park, as he had laid out the Parliament grounds in Toronto. Latham is responsible for most of the landscaping of the early Queens Park and was an organizer of the Royal Agricultural Society. He built a Victorian house for himself at **236 Third Street** in 1912, but didn't get much of a chance to enjoy it because he died that same year.

Westminster Brewery owner Nels Nelson moved to the area in 1912 and built what is now a massive peach-coloured timber and stone house at **127 Queens Avenue.** Originally from Denmark, Nelson went to sea at fourteen and eventually landed in Victoria where he decided to stay on terra firma and go into the beer business. He was the brew master at the Victoria and Nanaimo Breweries from 1866 to 1895 and then bought and merged the City and Westminster Breweries in 1897. Nels married Annette Sorenson, another Dane, in 1889, and they had six children. When he retired, he bought an orange grove in California and divided his time between the U.S. and his home in New Westminster. He died at the house in 1945. It sold soon after and met the fate of many of these mansions in the post-war housing shortage, becoming a sixteen-suite rooming house. It then changed hands several times, and the current owners, the Fields, bought the house in 1988 and have been renovating it ever since. "We put a lot of energy into being very true to the period," says Ethel Field. "When we finish something, we say to each other 'old Nels would be pleased with this.'"

Nearby, at **126 Granville Street,** is a rambling green Queen Anne Revival style house. An out building that looks like the original stables is now a garage. Both buildings sport matching stained glass windows designed by Henry Bloomfield and Sons. Richard Sharp, a former partner of Samuel Maclure's, designed the house in 1893 for Angus McColl, an enterprising lawyer who made Queens Counsel in 1892 and eventually Chief Justice. The house has huge half-circle windows that look out onto Queens Park. In the 1901 Census, Angus is forty-six, his wife Helen, thirty-six. They had two sons, oddly both named Angus: Angus Sholto born in 1889, and Angus Evan born in 1888. It also lists Soon, the domestic help, aged thirty-one. McColl died in 1902. Angus Evan died in May 1916, probably a war casualty, while the other Angus married Wenonah Mackenzie four months later in New Westminster.

In 1939, Bryon Johnson and his wife Kate built a very large brick Tudor Revival house on the corner of First Street at **101 Queens Avenue.** Born in 1890 in Victoria, Johnson was a professional lacrosse player in New Westminster and later he and his brother John started a construction supply company. Johnson went into politics in the '30s, becoming Premier in 1947 and serving for the next five years until WAC Bennett and the Socreds swept into power. Johnson is behind a controversial hospital insurance scheme and the provincial sales tax. The Johnsons only lived in the Queens Avenue house for about eight years before permanently moving to Victoria. The Way family owned the house for the next fifty-five years.

New Westminster raised its share of politicians, not surprising since it was the capital of the province until 1868. Still, New Westminster continued to develop as the principal city on the mainland with a thriving lumber and fishing industry. Many thought the fire of 1898 that destroyed so many of the city's businesses and houses would also destroy its spirit; but, undaunted, the citizens of New Westminster rebuilt.

Chapter 8

MOUNT PLEASANT: VANCOUVER'S FIRST SUBURB

Charles Ernest Bloomfield was twenty-one when his life changed one September evening. It was a typical Saturday night in New Westminster until just after 11:00 P.M. when, as one newspaper account described it, "Almost coincident with the ringing of the bell, a bright shower of sparks was seen to rise from the riverfront near the city market building. The clatter of hose carts along the almost deserted thoroughfares and the ringing of fire gongs rapidly filled the streets again, and the size of the blaze indicated surely enough to the southward hurrying crowds that the fire was going to be a big one."

The year was 1898.

Charles worked with his father Henry Bloomfield crafting art glass windows. Likely one of the few people with a camera, Charles watched and photographed the destruction of the downtown core and hundreds of houses, including his own home and business at Royal Avenue and Eighth Street.

"The noise was deafening," wrote a reporter. "Above the roar of the flames repeated explosions could be heard as the fire reached the different stocks of gunpowder, coal, and other explosive stores in the rich warehouses along Columbia and Front streets. The earth trembled with repeated shocks and the crash of breaking glass joined with the jar of falling walls to make the night a saturnalia horror."

On the Monday following the fire, the front page story of *The Province* screamed, "Gone up in a hell of roaring fire. The City of New Westminster practically wiped off the face of the earth. Upwards of two million dollars worth of property destroyed. All that is left of the business portion is a picturesque ruin. Hundreds of people are homeless."

While the city smouldered, Charles and his family moved to Vancouver.

THE BLOOMFIELDS

Henry and Emily Bloomfield and their three children James, Charles, and Ellen came to Canada from Maidenhead, England in 1889. Although the construction industry slowed to a virtual standstill through the 1890s depression, the Bloomfield's managed to win large contracts, including the stained glass for the Parliament buildings in Victoria, and the art glass for the Nanaimo Court House.

James, the eldest son, was away when the Great Fire hit. Since 1895, he had been working and studying in Chicago, New Orleans, Manchester, and London. By 1899, James had returned to Canada and the Bloomfield's lived at "Primrose House," a Queen Anne at the corner of West Tenth Avenue and Columbia Street. At that time, the address listed in the city directories was 169 West Tenth, later changing to **2544 Columbia Street**. While New Westminster was rebuilding, Mount Pleasant was little more than a village and just starting to see a housing boom after the arrival first of the railway, then of the streetcar in 1891.

The Bloomfield family home came with all the doodads of that period—the gingerbread trim, fish-scale shingles in the gables, finials on the gable tops, and, of course, stained and leaded glass windows throughout. Next door to the house, the Bloomfields built a much plainer blue Edwardian cottage with a basement for their studio. It was at this house at **2532 Columbia Street** that they created some of the most beautiful stained and leaded glass of the times. Work started to flow, and the Bloomfields laboured over numerous commissions for the houses of the moneyed gentry, such as Gabriola on Davie Street and Shaughnessy's Hycroft manor. The Queen Victoria window in St. Paul's Anglican Church in the West End is also their work.

The 1901 Census lists Henry Bloomfield, his wife Emily, and children James, twenty-eight, Charles, twenty-four, and Ellen, twenty-six all living at the house. Charles married Evelyn Pavier in November 1902, and that same year, commissioned über-architect Samuel Maclure to design a house (long since demolished) for fifteen hundred dollars on West Eighth Avenue. James married Mary Diamond in February 1903, and the following year, Ellen married Harry Tompson.

Now a skilled and sought after designer trained in watercolours and etching, James expanded his repertoire from tulips and roses to dogwood, trillium, skunk cabbage, and native art and cultural designs. His work caught the eye of Governor General Lord Aberdeen, and in 1903 James won the commission to create a modern version of Vancouver's official coat of arms.

The Bloomfield Studio, 2532 Columbia Street.
City of Vancouver Archives. Photo #SGN 423. Circa 1904.
Photographer: Charles E. Bloomfield

In 1936, Major Matthews, the archivist, recorded a conversation with Thomas Neelands who was mayor of Vancouver in 1902. He told Matthews about having James design the coat of arms. James apparently made two drawings. According to Neelands, the following year council started tinkering with the design. Apparently they shortened the fisherman's oilskin coat, made a change to the axe, and decided to add some balance by placing timber behind a lumberman to match an oar behind the fisherman.

James, horrified by this "alteration or two" by the councillors, wrote "complaining he had not been consulted," Neelands told Matthews. "But it did not make any difference. It appeared to us to be essentially no different from Mr. Blomfield's original design."

Henry Bloomfield retired in 1906, and James, who dropped an O to become James Blomfield, moved to the U.S. the following year.

After Bloomfield and Sons closed, Charles worked on a number of high profile commissions, including the leaded art glass for the Kamloops Courthouse and the stained glass heraldic windows in the great hall of the library at the University of British Columbia. From 1910 to 1912, he ran his own company, Vancouver Standard Glass. By 1906, Henry and Emily were well into their sixties and had moved to West Second Avenue. Emily died in 1910, and some time after her death Henry moved back to Mount Pleasant. He died in 1913.

By the turn of the century, Mount Pleasant had stores, a fire hall, nurseries, greenhouses, churches, and hundreds of new homes. It was largely a working class area where big houses sprung up on small lots. Henry Rae, shown as a shoe salesman in the directories, and his family were the next residents of the Bloomfield home. Next door at the studio, the house changed hands frequently. In 1905, the city directories list "Dennis," a woodworker, then by 1908, a carpenter with the delightful name of Jacob Tool. A second floor added around 1915 increased the size of the old Bloomfield studio to 1,700 square feet and gave the owner two more bedrooms and a bathroom. In 1920, the directories list Bell Pattison, an operator for B.C. Phones, as the occupant of the house.

While the succession of owners made extensive renovations to the Bloomfield home, the original studio remains relatively untouched. It still has the original room configuration, the high ceilings, the original glass light fixtures, and perfect first-growth fir floors, likely harvested from trees in the area. The front parlour, which looks west, has a piece of clear hexagonal leaded glass, and the dining room shows off fir wainscoting and a smart Victorian fireplace. A small niche contains two unusual pieces of Bloomfield stained-glass windows, sitting one on top of the other. The top piece has an intricate design of tulips and leaves in bold colours, while the bottom piece is a geometric design with more subdued blue tones. Possibly the windows were seconds rejected by clients, or perhaps panes that the Bloomfields felt were substandard.

In August 2005, the studio house went up for sale with a Heritage A sticker and an asking price of $750,000. Not surprisingly, considering its origins, the new owners have dug up a collection of broken pieces of stained glass in the garden.

THE DAVIS HOUSES

Across the road from the Bloomfield home, Robert Moore, a teamster, built his house at **166 West Tenth** in 1891, now one of the oldest surviving houses in Mount Pleasant. By 1900, the house sold to Joseph Donald, a grocery store proprietor. The longest residents

JOHN DAVIS HOUSE, 150 WEST 10 TH AVENUE.
THE HICKS FAMILY, CIRCA 1910.

in the house were Reverend A.W. Ward and his wife who lived there from 1926 until 1973 when the Davis family bought it and started to gradually transform the neighbourhood.

The Davis family paid thirty thousand dollars for the dilapidated Queen Anne house and set about restoring it. They installed new wiring and new plumbing, put on a new roof, did seismic upgrading, and redid the foundation and the framing. John senior, an engineer with Imperial Oil, drew up the plans, and his wife Pat took off all the woodwork, numbered it all, stripped it of layers of paint, and replaced it. "We saw a row of older houses that were untouched in Mount Pleasant, and nobody gave a damn about any of it at that time," says John Davis Jr. "We were seen to be the lunatic fringe."

Davis says others on the street bought speculative property in the hopes of seeing it transform into lucrative apartment buildings and were less than enthusiastic about the renovations. The Davis family ended up buying the house next door at **170 West Tenth**, renovating it and selling it to Ray Spaxman, then director of planning for the City of Vancouver. In 1977, four more heritage houses came up for sale on the block (**140, 144, 148** and **150**) as one basic building lot. Rather than see them evolve into yet another three-storey boxy apartment building, the Davis' borrowed a ton of money and started to redo them into apartments, all the while keeping an eye to the original historical detail. Next, **117 West Tenth**, now a bright orange Queen Anne, went up for sale, and close on its heels was **115 West Tenth,** now painted a cheerful purple. Soon after, John senior died from acute lymphocyte leukemia. The soaring interest rates of the '80s followed. "We were technically bankrupted by it," says his son.

"People who don't know us have the idea that we are some kind of aristocrats running around buying all these houses," says Davis. "They don't realize that it was all on borrowed money. We're not rich, just ordinary folk carrying all this debt all these years."

When an 1894 Queen Anne came up for sale at **156 West Tenth**, Davis and his mother managed to scrape up enough money to save it. All told, the family has helped bring back ten Queen Anne and Edwardian heritage houses on the block, all built between 1891 and 1910.

An oddity of Tenth Avenue is that the two Edwardians at 148 and 150 actually touch each other. Davis says a neighbour and descendant of one of the original families told him it was the result of a feud. "He said that two women came from England and had the house at 150 built right on the property line. That didn't offend the building code in 1907, if they even had such a thing, but it infuriated the owner of the property at 148 and he built his house the next year right up against their house in order to block the view out of the bay window on the side of 150, which he certainly achieved. I can attest to that."

Davis has a history written in 1981 by Joyce Sykes, a former resident of what she called "the cottage" at 144. In it she says that Fred Welsh was her landlord and owned at least three houses on the street. For as long as Sykes can recall, Welsh was well respected. She writes, "Mr. Welsh was a kindly man, but he did not mix with any of the neighbourhood; I doubt that he would know anyone by name, other than his own tenants." Welsh was a partner in Swartz Bros, a wholesale fruit and vegetable firm located in Gastown. He would leave for work at 4:30 A.M. every morning and arrive back in the afternoon. Sykes says he owned quite a bit of property in downtown Vancouver, including part of what eventually became Woodwards. In the 1930s, her father rented and operated two garages on his land.

Mrs. Welsh, says Sykes, was a member of several clubs and associations and held a strawberry tea garden party for charity every year. Weeks before the event, a Chinese gardener named Wong would come from the market garden in Marpole to get the roses into shape. "There were some awnings for the tea tables and lawn tables and benches," Sykes wrote. "Society ladies from all over Vancouver came; it was quite out of sync with the neighbourhood, where many families were on welfare. I recall ladies in long flowery dresses and carrying frilly parasols. They even kept their long white gloves on while they drank tea."

Davis says Welsh was a big wheel in those days. "I found his licence plates inside the wall from 1913; he had one of the first cars in this part of Vancouver." The barn at the back, where he kept his team of horses and wagon, is now a one bedroom apartment, which still has the original brick floor. Welsh lived on the street for almost half a century. While mostly trades people occupied the houses for the better part of the twentieth century, 140 had some colourful residents. When Davis bought the house, members of the Zen Centre of Vancouver lived there. "Really nice people," he says, adding that the only problem was they had a kitchen in the basement, and one day someone was cooking and set the curtains on fire. "Holy smoke, we just about lost that house," he says. "If the fire department hadn't come straight away it would have been a goner."

LADNER HOUSE

In 1899, George A. Miller built a Victorian home around the corner from the Davis houses at **2647 Manitoba Street.** It's called the Ladner house, which is odd, since there is only a tenuous connection to the Ladner family. The first resident to show up in the house, according to the city directories, is a William B. Steinner (retired) in 1902. William Booth Skinner appears in the directories two years later. Skinner ran a boot and shoe store on Westminster Avenue, now Main Street, and he and his wife Kate had three daughters. Valerie Grant, who traced the Ladner family history, says that William inherited part of his grandfather William Booth's property in Delta in 1887. Records show that Skinner married in New Westminster district in 1884. The main connection to the Ladner family is that Skinner's aunts Mary Ann and Edna Booth married Thomas Ellis Ladner and William Henry Ladner respectively, the brothers who went on to develop the community that bears their name. Once a single family home, the Manitoba Street house is now divided into apartments, but the building has kept its historical features and a huge copper beech tree imported from Belgium still sits in the front yard. Grant thinks the Beech tree was a gift from Leon Ladner, Thomas Ladner's son who married Jeanne Lantzius in Brussels in 1912.

GRACE MACINNIS

Grace MacInnis, the woman who blazed trails as a politician, lived nearby at **442 West Fifteenth Avenue.** City directories have her and husband Angus, a long-time NDP MP, living at the large cream-coloured Georgian house from the late 1940s to 1955. Grace's father, James Woodsworth, formed the Cooperative Commonwealth Federation Party in 1932. When he died a decade later, Bruce Hutchison wrote in *The Vancouver Sun,* "He was the most Christ-like man ever seen in Parliament, and his white beard, his flaming eye, his anger at injustice, his gentleness with everyone, and his deep, booming voice of moral protest made him appear like a prophet out of the Old Testament. He was the saint in our politics."

No surprise, really, that Grace, the oldest of six children, who was born into politics, grew up on politics, and married into politics, would become a politician. Grace worked as her father's secretary in Ottawa and married Angus MacInnis, a labour MP from Vancouver, the following year. In the '30s, she fought for birth control when it was still illegal to provide contraception. She fought for income for stay-at-home mothers in the 1940s and in 1941 ran as the CCF member for Vancouver/Burrard and won. She lost the seat in the next election four years later, but remained a force within the party and a strong voice against the internment of Japanese Canadians during the Second World War. She published a biography of her father in 1953, and when Angus died in 1964, returned to politics, winning the Vancouver-Kingsway seat for the federal NDP the following year to become BC's first female MP. During that decade she campaigned for women's rights to abortion. In 1974 at the age of sixty-nine, she resigned her seat because of severe arthritis.

GRAUER HOUSE

Jacob Grauer, one of the city's early pioneers, lived at **364 West Tenth Avenue** in a 1909 house that's a mix of Queen Anne and Edwardian styles. An almost identical house sits at 1829 Parker Street in the Grandview-Woodlands area, and it's likely the design came from a pattern book. In 1996, developers saved the West Tenth house, but added condominiums to the grounds. The house, still beautiful with its shingled exterior and leaded windows, would have given the Grauer's a stunning view of the North Shore Mountains when they lived there in the early 1900s.

A German immigrant, Grauer left home at eighteen travelling first to New York and gradually making his way to Seattle. He married Marie Neth, who came from his hometown in Wurtemberg, in 1883 and set about buying lambs in Washington and selling them in British Columbia. The enterprising Grauer's moved to Vancouver in 1886, expanded their farming operation to include cattle, started a butcher shop called City Market on Cordova Street, and raised nine children. In the mid-1890s, he bought and cleared three hundred acres of land near Eburne (roughly where the Vancouver International Airport is now), ran the Eburne post office and general store, and, in 1900, bought another six hundred and forty acres near Ladner for raising sheep.

A book called *The History of Germans in Canada* tells a story about Grauer and the B.C. Electric Company. "In June 1907 Jake, as Grauer was known, was injured in a tram accident and the following March he sued the company for fifteen thousand dollars." It's a tad ironic, because Grauer's son Dal eventually became head of B.C. Electric, the forerunner to B.C. Hydro.

In an article written after Grauer retired, an unnamed writer waxes, "Jacob Grauer is living retired in Vancouver after many years of close identification with its business interests and those of Eburne and Steveston and with the agricultural development of this part of the province. He is one of the wealthy men of Vancouver and has made his success entirely unaided, as he came to America a poor boy with unwavering determination." The article talks about how the sons will take over the farms and how six younger children, including Albert Edward (Dal) are still at school and living at 364 Tenth Avenue, "a well-appointed modern home."

Grauer died in 1936 at the age of seventy-six, before Dal's daughter Sherry Grauer was born. "It's all pretty legendary to me," she says. "Grandpa Grauer was the person who organized getting dykes built on Sea Island. It was Grandma Grauer who amazes me. I once spoke to a woman who had been a telephone operator in Marpole. My grandfather had his butcher's shop there and eventually owned the building. The telephone exchange was upstairs. She told me that Grandma Grauer was here at all hours and she'd be rocking the cradle with one foot and chopping the sauerkraut at the same time. My Aunt Marie told me that one of the glorious memories that she remembers is that when she was young she got to drive the pony cart up and down the shores of the Fraser delivering meat."

PERCY WILLIAMS

As Jacob Grauer's thoughts led to retirement, another Mount Pleasant resident put Vancouver on the world's sporting map. Percy Williams, born in 1908, lived at **196 West Twelfth Avenue** from 1928 to 1940. Williams, a scrawny kid, weighing one hundred and ten pounds, with a bad heart from childhood rheumatic fever, was "discovered" at King Edward High School at age eighteen. An article at the *Historica* Web Site says Coach Bob Granger took on Williams after he tied with his sprint champion in 1926, "violating every known principle of the running game."

Granger had interesting training techniques. His idea of warming Williams up was having him lie on the dressing table under a pile of blankets. Another was making him run flat out into a mattress propped against a wall. Unorthodox maybe, but Williams kept winning. By 1928, the five-foot-six-inch kid had bulked up to 125 pounds and won two gold medals for the two hundred and one hundred metre sprints at the Amsterdam Olympics. The newspapers dubbed him "Peerless Percy," and he returned to Vancouver to a welcome from 40,000 people. Kids got the day off school and one firm came out with an "Our Percy" chocolate bar.

A reluctant star, it was with mixed relief when, in 1932, a leg injury ended his track career. Later, he told a reporter, "Oh, I was so glad to get out of it all." By 1935, the public had forgotten Williams, and city directories show him working as a salesman for Armstrong and Laing. Later, he ran an insurance business. In 1982, suffering from arthritis, he shot himself in his bathtub.

One of many interesting things about Mount Pleasant is the crazy pattern of streets east of Ontario Street. Instead of the orderly grid system, this area is a maze of streets that don't line up, end abruptly, start wide and finish not much bigger than a skinny lane, and houses that sit right to the edge of the street, jammed onto tiny lots.

John Atkin, local author, gives walking tours of Vancouver neighbourhoods. He has an intimate familiarity both with the big picture and with the details of architecture: he can tell the difference between a dentil and a cantilever. "Before the 1929 amalgamation of South Vancouver and Point Grey, South Vancouver did whatever they wanted," he says. "Houses face in different directions on different size lots. Quebec Street doesn't line up; Twenty-second has a different width." Part of the problem, says Atkin, was when South Vancouver went broke around 1918 the city government allowed residents to do their own road improvements in lieu of taxes."

LEDINGHAM HOUSE

Peter Fenton, a contractor who lived in Mount Pleasant for close to a decade, originally at 348 East Eighth Avenue, changed to **2425 Brunswick Street**, built the Ledingham House in 1895. The Queen Anne house, takes its name from its more prominent tenant George W. Ledingham. He bought the house shortly after his return from the Boer War and lived there with his wife Helen and three children until his death in 1942 at age sixty-seven. In 1905 he worked as foreman of concrete construction for the city and eventually partnered up with C.E. Cooper, a consulting engineer. Together they laid several hundred miles of Vancouver's concrete sidewalk.

Before marrying George in 1903, Helen Reavely of Ontario was an embalmer at her father's undertaking business. She rates a paragraph in a three-page biography of Ledingham. "She has decided business qualifications and is a great help to her husband, who discusses with her often his business transactions and profits by her sound advice. An excellent wife and mother, she has created a home atmosphere which is happy in every respect and she hospitably entertains the many friends of the family. She is popular in social circles on account of her many accomplishments and is a favourite in the best homes of the city."

The yellow Queen Anne with the top floor turret that looks out on the North Shore Mountains is now part of a housing development called Ledingham Place. It has a sidewalk that sweeps around the block—possibly built by Ledingham himself.

CHARLES BENTALL

The man who shaped much of Vancouver's city skyline lived for more than a decade at a humble stuccoed house at **469 East Tenth Avenue.** Born in England in 1881, Charles Bentall left school at thirteen, trained as an engineer, and then immigrated first to Ontario and then to Vancouver in 1908. He was deeply religious, active in the Baptist Church, and founded the local Kiwanis Club and the Vancouver Better Business Bureau. In 1915, as an engineer for Dominion Construction, he worked on the World Tower, later known as the Sun Tower. After the last girder was bolted into place, Bentall apparently shimmied up the nineteen floors of steel structure, bowed his head, said a prayer of thanks that no workers were killed, and gave a blessing for all those who would work inside what was then the tallest office tower in the British Empire.

The following year, Bentall became general manager of Dominion, and by 1920, he owned the company. B.T. Rogers hired Dominion to lay the concrete foundation for Shannon, his mansion, in 1914. Rogers died in 1918, and it took his wife, Mary Rogers, another seven years to complete Shannon. When she left Gabriola in 1925, she had Bentall convert the mansion into apartments. That December, a notation in her diary says she sold her interest in the Angus Apartments at Gabriola to Bentall for twenty-five thousand dollars. Directories show that Charles and his wife Edna lived at the Mount Pleasant address until 1936. Two years later, it lists them as living at 206, 1531 Davie Street.

By the time Charles retired eight years later, his fingerprints were everywhere: the domed roof of the old Vancouver courthouse; the art deco Capitol Theatre; Point Grey Secondary School; the Rogers Sugar Refinery building; two Jewish synagogues; and later, the B.C. Pavilion at Expo 86 and the Bentall office towers in downtown Vancouver. Charles' sons, Clark and Robert, ran the company for almost three decades until a family feud split it up in 1988. Charles lived at his Angus Apartment until he died at ninety one in 1974. In 1986, the Canadian Business Hall of Fame added his name to its exclusive list of members.

PETER PANTAGES

At the same time that Charles and Edna Bentall lived on East Tenth, another intriguing individual lived nearby at **343 East 13th Avenue**. Peter Basil Pantages kicked off the Polar

Bear swim on January 1, 1920, about a year after he'd arrived in Vancouver from Greece. Pantages first started work as an usher at his cousin Alexander's Pantages' Theatre on Hastings Street. By 1929, he was running the Peter Pan Café on Granville with his three brothers Lloyd, Angelo, and Alphonsos.

The house on East Thirteenth backs onto busy Kingsway and sits next door to a Speedy Glass franchise. It's a plain yellow three-storey house that would have once looked identical to its next door Queen Anne style neighbour. Unfortunately owners have stripped or "modernized" the house over the years. City directories have Peter, brother Angelo, listed as a waiter, and their mother, Adamandia Pantages living there in 1925. Peter married Helen Sarantis in 1930, and they brought up four kids in the house. The family lived there until the 1970s.

Known to swim in English Bay three times a day, every day, Pantages wanted everyone to know that it was possible to swim every day of the year in Vancouver. The story goes that he invited a handful of mates over for a New Year's drink and talked them into taking the plunge into the waters of English Bay. That event kicked off the Polar Bear Club. Under the constitution of the club, anyone who wanted to be president had to go swimming every day—no freezing rain, snow, or sickness excused. It's likely that the daily swimming requirement meant that Pantages was president for most of his life. Still, the Polar Bear Swim now attracts up to 2,000 people, including his own grandchildren. Up to 10,000 Vancouverites make it an annual spectator sport.

Peter died in Hawaii in 1971; he'd been swimming, of course. The café outlasted him by a few years, operating for more than four decades in all. Helen died in 1973 at age sixty-four.

JIMMY CUNNINGHAM

Next time you're walking along the Stanley Park seawall, spare a thought for Jimmy Cunningham, the stonemason who built over five kilometres of the nearly nine kilometre wall during his lifetime. He would be devastated to learn of the damage to his seawall after wind storms hit the park in December 2006, knocking down thousands of trees and causing extensive damage to the asphalt surface and the foundations beneath the seawall.

The building of the wall started in 1917 and at times had more than twenty-three hundred men working on it. But Cunningham, who stood five feet, four inches tall, spent thirty-two years heaving granite blocks weighing hundreds of pounds into place. A Scot, he immigrated to Vancouver in 1910 and became master stonemason for the Parks Board in 1931.

From 1921 until he retired in 1955, Cunningham, his wife Elizabeth, and their three daughters lived at **4446 Quebec Street,** a tree-lined street near Nat Bailey Stadium in an established neighbourhood of Queen Annes and Edwardian houses just above Mount Pleasant. The Cunningham house is painted teal and has a large bay window and welcoming front porch. Surprisingly—considering his occupation—instead of a stone fence, there's a well-kept hedge.

Cunningham's granddaughter, Julia Flather Murrell, says her grandfather would talk to her in Gaelic. She remembers a big potbellied stove in the kitchen and having to boil water for the upstairs bath. During her nursing training, she would often meet her grandfather at the seawall and remembers his gnarled, swollen hands. "His right hand was really quite swollen and almost deformed because of all the cutting all those years," she says. "He never stopped working on the wall. They lowered him down on the rope at low tide and he chose the rock to be cut and cut the rock right down on the beach. He did all the work himself. And he was still doing that into his eighties."

Stuart Lefeaux, a civil engineer and manager of the Parks Board, masterminded much of the layout of the wall. He retired in 1978.

"Jimmy ran all of our crews building that wall; he was the master mason," says Lefeaux. "In those days, stone masonry was a big part of building, not just seawalls."

Lefeaux says most of the granite blocks came from the beach, the city streets, and a stone quarry on Nelson Island, but he says a few of them are abandoned headstones from Mountain View Cemetery. "Wherever we could get stone, especially granite, we would send out our trucks and machinery and pick them up," he says.

Long after Cunningham hung up his trowel, he'd head down to supervise the crew building the seawall. He died in 1963 at the age of eighty-five, seventeen years before completion of his seawall. Jimmy and Elizabeth Cunningham, who died within months of each other, had their ashes buried behind the rock at Siwash Rock. There's a plaque in his name there, and every October, the James Cunningham Seawall Race takes place. Every year up to eight million people visit Stanley Park, and on summer weekends, more than a thousand people walk Cunningham's seawall every hour. "He would chuckle and enjoy that," says Lefeaux.

While the Bloomfields and other early residents of Mount Pleasant might recognize some of their old homes, they'd be shocked at the way the city developed. No longer a village, Mount Pleasant is now part of the urban sprawl. Up Main Street between Broadway and Sixteenth Avenue are Chinese, Vietnamese, Cambodian, Japanese, Russian, and Hungarian restaurants. Fresh paint, often in authentic heritage colours, gives a nostalgic feel to the vintage clothing stores, antique shops, and hundred-plus-year-old houses that survived the '50s and '60s apartment boom. Along West Tenth, the flower beds that spill out onto the street spruce up the ugly low-rise apartments. Typical of how the new butts up against the old, there is a sign outside a renovated turn of the century house on West Tenth near Manitoba. The sign points to where Brewery Creek once ran and supplied both Charles Doering and the Reifel's breweries "beer without a peer" with water.

Chapter 9

MURDEROUS MAYHEM

Like all good cities, Vancouver has had its share of murders. Some are mysterious, some are movie of the week material, and still others are just plain tragic. The murders that follow span half a century and all took place in family homes in Greater Vancouver. Only one of the murders remains unsolved. All the houses still stand and range from a modest Eastside bungalow to a rambling mansion.

JANET SMITH

The Janet Smith murder rocked Vancouver's elite and fascinated the masses. The murder touched on high-level police corruption, kidnapping, drugs, rumoured society orgies, and rampant racism.

In 1924, Janet Smith was found shot in the head by a .45 calibre automatic revolver in the basement of **3851 Osler Avenue** in the upmarket Shaughnessy Heights. A pretty twenty-two-year-old Scottish nanny, Smith worked for Fred Baker who was living in his brother's house while he was overseas. Richard Baker's wife, Blanche, was the daughter of the very rich and influential Alexander Duncan McRae who lived close by at Hycroft manor.

Fred Baker moved from Vancouver to London to run an import-export business in 1920. While in London, he hired Janet Smith to look after his baby daughter. As Scotland Yard became increasingly suspicious of Fred Baker's "pharmaceutical" business, the Baker's moved to Paris taking Janet along. In 1923, they all moved back to Vancouver.

Police botched the Smith case. First it took two days to find the bullet. Then the embalming of her body destroyed evidence at the eventual autopsy. Police called it suicide in the face of overwhelming evidence that it wasn't. Evidence from Fred Baker at the first inquest said he believed that she'd found his brother's army automatic that he'd kept in a bag in the front hall, and overcome with curiosity, decided to give it a close look. As Eric Nicol writes in *Vancouver*, "This implied that the girl had interrupted her ironing to come upstairs, remove the fully loaded revolver from the haversack, return to the basement and accidentally pull the trigger with the gun aimed at her head."

The inquest ruled it accidental death. But the police finally clued in that there were no powder burns around the bullet hole, and unless she also beat herself in the back of the head, burned herself on the back with the iron, and changed her clothes after she was dead, her death was no accident. The newspaper headline changed to, "Smith Girl Murdered."

Wong Foon Sing, the Chinese houseboy who heard the shot while he peeled potatoes in the kitchen, found her in a pool of blood, and naturally was the logical fall guy. Police interrogated him for several hours. Pressure from the Scottish community increased. Smith's body was dug up and a second inquest was held in late August. In a story from *The Province* in 1980, Chuck Davis writes that there was nearly a riot outside the Georgia Street courtroom as hundreds turned up looking for a seat. "The crush was so great that C.W. Craig, K.C., the lawyer representing the Attorney General, had to climb on someone's shoulders and call through the transom above the locked door of the court to be let in."

During the investigation, police conducted an experiment that puts the TV show *CSI* to shame. They got their hands on an unclaimed head from the local mental hospital and fired bullets into its brain.

In one of the many bizarre turns in the case, on March 20, 1925, several men dressed in Ku Klux Klan robes and hoods kidnapped the Chinese houseboy. At one point, they beat him so hard in their exuberance to force a confession, that they ruptured his ear drum. The kidnappers dragged Wong to an attic, tied a heavy rope around his neck, put him on a stool, and pretended to kick it out from under him. After a staggering six weeks of torture, they dumped him in the middle of the night. Police found him stumbling along Marine Drive.

Wong didn't catch a break. Police arrested him and shipped him off to Oakalla prison to await trial. The trial kept the story on the front page of the newspapers, and allegations that Fred Baker was involved in drug smuggling and a suspect in the murder, fed the media frenzy. Baker admitted under questioning that his export company handled heroin, cocaine, and morphine. Baker added that Janet Smith had nothing to do with his business and he never stored drugs at his house.

Racial tensions raged as Vancouver's Chinese community demanded answers. Then during Wong's murder trial, police arrested several men for his kidnapping. Those arrested included several highranking members of the Point Grey Police Department and the head of something called the Canadian Detective Agency.

The jury acquitted Wong and he left for China in March 1926.

The murder of Janet Smith remains unsolved, but over the years armchair detectives have come up with a couple of different scenarios. Some say it was Fred Baker, the employer, who killed Smith to hide his drug use and business dealings. Others say a scenario was devised to cover up her rape and murder at a wild society party, after which the murderer, or a close associate, dragged her body to Osler Street to throw off the investigation. Still others suggested it was Jack Nichol, son of Walter Nichol, lieutenant-governor and publisher of *The Province*. However, that was highly unlikely as he was out of town at the time of the murder. Few think it was the Chinese houseboy.

Smith's body rests uneasily at Mountain View Cemetery, buried by Vancouver's Scots. Around the corner from the headstone are some coins put there to pay the "ferry man" for Janet's safe passage to the afterlife.

ESTHER CASTELLANI

The green duplex at **2092 West Forty-second Avenue** just off East Boulevard is such an ordinary place, set in this middle class, mostly retirement community, that's it's hard to imagine it was the stage for one of the most sensational murders in Vancouver's history.

Esther Castellani, aged forty, died July 11, 1965 from months of arsenic poisoning that had gone undetected during several doctor's visits and a two-month hospital stay. City directories show that while Rene and Esther Castellani moved frequently, they lived in the duplex between 1963 and 1965. Rene was a minor radio personality making around fifty-two hundred dollars a year with CKNW and Esther worked as a saleswoman at Miss J.S. Dayton, a children's clothing store in Kerrisdale. They'd been married nineteen years and had a twelve-year-old daughter.

It wasn't until three weeks after she died that Ted Fennell, the city analyst discovered the cause of her death. He tipped off the police that he had found levels of arsenic in her hair and finger nails that were up to fifteen hundred times the normal arsenic content of the body. It took police months to collect enough evidence to charge Rene with murder. The final piece was the Triox weed killer containing fifty-three percent arsenic still under the kitchen sink. A lethal dose would be a mere three to five drops. Three fluid ounces

of the concentrate were missing from the can. While Esther thought her husband was trying to encourage her to eat, he was actually spooning weed killer into her White Spot milk
shakes.

Rene didn't take the stand at the first trial, which was surprising since he'd proven himself a good actor. His first stunt for CKNW's promotion department was to play a
Maharaja intent on buying the province of British Columbia—even going so far as to take
out ads on bus boards. He stayed at the Western Bayshore, dressed in fancy costumes befit-
ting an Indian prince, rode around in limousines with bodyguards, and had an entourage
of dancing girls. So effective was the campaign that people made signs shouting, "Keep
B.C. British." In another campaign to beef up ratings, Rene played the "Dizzy Dialer,"
doing a radio version of "Candid Camera." His last ingenious stunt for the station before
Esther's death was climbing to the top of the twenty-metre Bow Mac sign on West Broadway
and vowing to stay there until every last car on the lot sold. It took eight days.

At the trial, Rene's lawyer stupidly denied that his client was having an affair with the
radio station's receptionist, a young widow named Adelaide Ann Miller (Lolly). Her husband had drowned while the two were boating a few years before and left her $25,000. It
was common knowledge at the station that Rene was seeing the blonde receptionist outside
of the office. Bill Hughes, station manager, asked for her resignation, and, ironically, the
only reason Castellani hung onto his job was because Hughes knew he had a sick wife.

Apparently, even Esther knew or guessed of the affair. She'd received anonymous late-
night phone calls from a woman who would ask, "Do you know your husband is going
around with someone else, a woman named Lolly?" And she also found a love letter from
Lolly in Rene's pocket. A few months after she confronted him, she started to get sick with
stomach and lower back pain severe enough to keep her off work. Over the next couple of
months, she had bouts of nausea and diarrhea which quickly turned into intense stomach
pains and vomiting. In May, a doctor made a house call and gave her an injection of Gravol
and Demerol to curb the pain. Various diagnoses had the cause as sodium retention or
gallbladder or gastric problems brought on by poor diet.

Rene ramped up the poison, spoon feeding it into her in her food and drink. Esther's
health got steadily worse. Her fingers and toes went numb, and she couldn't walk or use
her hands.

A few weeks before Esther died, Rene and Lolly told a builder and a real-estate agent
that they were going to be married. The day after her funeral, Rene and Lolly met with a
bank manager, and the next day they packed up the kids (Rene's daughter, Jeannine, and
Lolly's six-year-old), and took off for a two-week holiday to Disneyland.

The family pressured Rene into agreeing to an autopsy. The coroner found Esther had ingested arsenic for six to thirteen months before her death, including the time she was in hospital. The lab charted the amount of arsenic Esther received day by day, using a strand of her long black hair. What helped to convict Rene was that for the eight days he was sitting up on the Bow Mac sign, there wasn't any sign of arsenic poisoning in her hair growth.

Three months after Esther's death, CKNW fired Rene and soon after, police arrested him for capital murder, just two days after he and Lolly applied for a marriage license. The jury found him guilty on February 21, 1967 and sentenced him to hang. The following month he was granted a new trial by the appeal court, and this time decided to plead his case and admitted to adultery. When he was found guilty for the second time, Rene turned to the twelve jurors and said, "May God have mercy on *your* souls."

His death sentence was commuted to life imprisonment, and the system paroled him in 1979. Lolly, by this time, had remarried. Rene worked at KFVR Abbotsford for a while and then moved to Nanaimo to help launch CKEG where he was known as "Rene the Roadrunner" because he drove around town passing out promotional gifts. Rene eventually remarried and died of cancer in 1982.

THE KOSBERG FAMILY

Just off Main Street, the little house at **142 East Twenty-second Avenue** looks innocent, but it was the scene of one of Vancouver's grisliest murders. On December 9, 1965, the house had a bright Santa Claus painted on the front window. But just as Osborne and Dorothy Kosberg and their children, fifteen-year-old Barry, thirteen-year-old Marianne, eleven-year-old Gayle, and two-year-old Vincent were thinking of Christmas, their oldest brother was planning their violent murders. Seventeen-year-old Thomas had a history of mental illness, but no one could see him plotting a murder, let alone drugging his family and hacking them to bits with a double-bladed axe.

On the night of the murder, Thomas bought a bottle of twenty-five sleeping pills from a local drugstore. He made chocolate milkshakes for his mother, four siblings, and Florence, a family friend who was visiting and watching television with the family. Florence sat at one end of the chesterfield while Thomas sat at the other reading a book. She remembers Dorothy saying, "I didn't know that I was that tired." Florence fell asleep and woke up about 11:00 P.M. She had difficulty staying awake and Thomas suggested she stay the night, but she called a taxi and left. Thomas waited up for Osborne, a driver for Allied Heat and Fuel who was working a late shift. He too got a milkshake. After Osborne was asleep, Thomas went to the basement and came back upstairs with the axe. After hacking up his family, he drove off in the family's 1954 sedan and ran it into a power pole. He talked a family friend into giving him a ride to the West Vancouver home of his former psychiatrist, Dr. Wong. Police described him as "neatly dressed" and "calm" when they picked him up.

When police kicked in the front door of the Kosberg's house just before 8:00 A.M., veteran officer Superintendent James Mundie told a reporter that the scene inside the house was the worst crime of violence he had seen in his long career. The bodies of Osborne and Dorothy were in the bedroom. In a crib beside their bodies was baby Vincent. Vincent had escaped the axe, and survived a strangulation attempt, but Barry died in a back bedroom, and police found the body of Gayle and her injured sister Marianne in a front bedroom.

Marianne underwent emergency surgery for head wounds but died days later.

At the February 1967 trial, two psychiatrists told the court that Thomas was a schizophrenic, quite capable of carrying out a "complex and deliberate plan" but not capable of distinguishing whether what he was doing was right or wrong. To no one's surprise, the court ruled Thomas not guilty by reason of insanity and shipped him off to Riverview.

THE WEBERS

On February 17, 1970, Karl Weber went to the front door of his Champlain Heights bungalow and took a shot to the chest. As he lay on the floor, his murderer bent down and shot him again execution style in the back of the head. Lieselotte Weber, his wife, alerted by the gun shots, came out of the bathroom, turned and yelled at her nine-year-old daughter Diane to run. A terrified Diane watched the visitor shoot her mother. As with her father, Diane saw the gun man lean over her mother's body and shoot her in the back of the head.

Diane ran out of the house screaming. She reached a neighbour's house and started hammering on the door. Another neighbour looked out of the window and saw a man wearing dark clothing come out the front door, run down the side of the house, and disappear. She phoned police.

City directories list Karl Weber as a painter who worked for A.C. Rogers and Sons. The Webers immigrated from Germany and had lived in Canada since the mid-'50s. The year of the murder, they lived in a bungalow at **6383 Brooks Avenue**, a working class neighbourhood with dozens of identical bungalows in the area. Police soon found that there was nothing routine about this murder.

Joe Swan, a former Vancouver Police Sergeant wrote in his book *Police Beat: 24 Vancouver Murders* that Diane Weber later told police on the day of the murder she was watching her favourite television show "Mod Squad." Her mother was running a bath, and her father was sitting in a chair reading the newspaper. A little after 8:00 P.M., her mother answered the front door. She called out, "Karl, there's someone to see you." Diane saw a man with dark hair, wearing a green rubberized coat. She saw the man pull a "gangster gun" from his coat, and she heard gunshots.

A search of the area by police and their dogs failed to turn up any trace of the shooter. They did manage to recover ten .22 calibre bullets in the hallway and from the bodies. They figured it for an underworld hit.

What surprised police, writes Swan, was that the family owned expensive furnishings that seemed out of place in the small house. The master bedroom had expensive Spanish style furniture. They found a second bedroom in the basement decked out in a Hawaiian theme, with one entire wall covered in large mirrors. Next door to this room was a rec room with a large, well-stocked bar. Police found expensive stereo, tape-recording, film, and other photographic equipment. Photographs, films, and letters showed that the Webers were involved in suburban wife swapping. Neighbours told of men dropping in to see the forty-one-year-old, for twenty-minute visits when Karl wasn't home. One neighbour handed police a list of fifty-nine license plate numbers, complete with dates, times, and duration of visits.

Police found that Lieselotte once lived in the West End with two other prostitutes and called herself "Yvonne." One of the women was married to a heroin trafficker, and the police investigation went from prostitution and blackmail to drugs. A month after the murder, they did another sweep of the Weber house and this time found $4,610 in fifty, twenty, and ten-dollar bills behind a valance wall in the basement, along with small pieces of paper with various street addresses and notations that the drug squad immediately recognized as notes telling customers where to find their drugs. The notes led police to eight hundred caps of heroin buried in glass jars under telephone poles and fence posts.

Police now followed the connections between the Webers and the drug war. Two days before their shooting, police found Leslie Irwin, a forty-one-year-old addict and dealer from North Vancouver, behind the wheel of his Lincoln Continental, shot to death from a shotgun blast.

Weeks later, police informants led police to the murder weapon and to the killer: Murray Boyd, who had escaped from the B.C. Penitentiary on the nineteenth of January. He was paid one thousand dollars for the three hits. Police linked the murders to a struggle between two syndicates for control of the Vancouver hard-drug trade.

The case never went to trial. Vancouver detectives shot Boyd to death on April 21, 1970 while he sat in his truck. On May 4, following a tip, police divers found a sawed-off shotgun in the water off Prospect Point in Stanley Park.

Two months after the Weber's murder, police found Jacqueline Anne Lampen, a twenty-seven-year-old exotic dancer shot in the chest and left leg with the same twenty-two-calibre rifle that killed the Webers. She died in the basement of her Burnaby home.

Police charged twenty-one-year-old Andrew Graydon Bruce with the murder. A convicted drug dealer and associate of Bruce's told police that he had driven Bruce to Oxford Street on April 19. He also told them where to look for the gun, and that he had seen a gun just like it in Bruce's bedroom. The theory went that Boyd had subcontracted the hit to Bruce.

Crown prosecutor Stewart Chambers told the court, "This killing was highly efficient and expert. This was a killing of someone not previously known to the accused." Arguing that his client should get bail, Terry Robertson told the judge, "It's not as if he was brought in from Chicago to bump somebody off. This is perhaps a bit of overkill on the part of the police."

No doubt there were few dry eyes when seven-year-old Cheryl Ann Lampen took the stand. Clutching a stuffed shaggy blue dog, she told the court how she was watching television around 9:00 P.M. on the Sunday night when a man came to the door and asked to see her mother. The man, she said, told her his name was John. Cheryl Ann said the man and her mother looked in several closets, drawers, and cupboards and went down the basement stairs. "I heard them talking. Then the man shot her," she told the judge. "I heard two bangs."

Bruce got a life sentence.

PATRICIA LOWTHER

Patricia Lowther died in September 1975, beaten to death in her home at **566 East Forty-sixth Avenue** in Vancouver. A noted, but fairly obscure poet with a lover and a jealous husband, Lowther, for a time, was far more famous in death.

Lowther, forty-two, grew up in North Vancouver and spent her life on the West Coast. She started writing poetry as a small child and, according to a biography, had her first poem published in *The Vancouver Sun* when she was ten. She had two children from her first marriage in 1953, then married Lowther in 1963 and had two more children. She published her first collection of poems in 1968. Her most well-known work was *A Stone Diary* published by Oxford University Press after her death.

At the time of the murder, fifty-one-year-old Roy Lowther was a failed poet and a school teacher who, for over a decade, worked for a least three school districts in Maple Ridge, Coquitlam, and Delta. By the early '70s, he stopped teaching altogether. He was married once before and spent two months in Essondale Hospital after assaulting his first wife. They divorced in 1963, and he married Pat that same year.

The mustard-coloured house where they lived near Mountain View Cemetery is an old, three-storey, classic kit home with a welcoming front porch and stained glass on the front door. A church graces the end of the street and the pleasant neighbourhood seems like a place where bad things just don't happen.

A week after she'd last seen her mother, Kathy Domphousse went to police and reported her missing. Kathy's stepfather, Roy Lowther, told her that Patricia had left three days before to go back east somewhere and didn't know when she'd be back. Kathy was immediately suspicious. Her mother hadn't mentioned travelling and, as co-chair of the League of Canadian Poets, was in the middle of organizing a major poetry conference in Victoria. She was also teaching a senior workshop at the University of B.C.'s creative writing department, and it was quite out of character for her to go away and leave her students in the lurch.

Roy told police that his wife was having an affair with a poet in Ontario, and he assumed Patricia had gone there to be with him. He said they'd gone to bed together on September 24, 1975, but when he woke up the next morning Patricia was gone. Police checked airlines, and rail and bus companies, but no one, including Eugene McNamara, the Ontario poet, had seen her.

On October 13, a family hiking at Furry Creek found a body lying face down in the water, its head and shoulders jammed under a log. The body was badly decomposed and police identified Lowther from fingerprints and dental records. An autopsy found the cause of death was a severe blow to the back of the neck so hard that it had smashed in her skull.

Lowther and his two children had gone to stay at their house on Mayne Island after Patricia went missing. It was there that police found a recently washed blood-stained mattress and a hammer, both brought from the house on Forty-sixth Avenue. A search of the couple's bedroom found one hundred and seventeen blood spots on the wall.

Lowther's lawyers put up a fascinating defence. Roy admitted finding his wife's naked, battered body in the upstairs bedroom. He said he assumed one of her lovers had murdered her, and that as the husband, police would suspect him. He decided to get rid of the body. First, he stowed her body on a chair in an unlocked closet so his two young daughters wouldn't see it, then at 3:00 A.M., he carried it down the back stairs and out to the trunk of the car. He went back to the bedroom to pick up the bloodstained mattress and the clothes he'd used to wipe the blood from the walls and ceilings. Finally, he drove to Furry Creek, just a few miles from where he'd grown up at Britannia Beach, threw his wife's body over a cliff and hoped it would stay hidden. "It dropped away and came to rest on a rock about three feet above the waters of the stream," Lowther told the jury, adding that he expected the body to stay there during the winter snow until the spring. But rain caused the creek to rise higher, and the body floated down the creek.

As Lowther took the stand in his own defence, a reporter described him as unhealthy looking. "With his pale complexion and narrow stooped shoulders, Lowther, at fifty-two, could easily pass for sixty-five. His ill-fitting grey suit jacket—perhaps it was once a royal blue—hangs on his frame like a burlap sack and the doubled-up folds in his waistline suggest a drastic loss of weight."

The lover, McNamara, is described by the same reporter as a chunky Ernest Hemingway—a short, rumpled intellectual. "He is academically fashionable in an unfashionable checkered tweed sports coat, looking conspicuously distant, obviously uncomfortable with the entire affair."

The jury convicted Roy Lowther of his wife's murder in June 1977. He died in prison in 1985, two years before coming up for parole. In 1980, the League of Canadian Poets established the annual Pat Lowther award to honour a new book by a Canadian woman poet.

MARION HAMILTON

When police found the body of Marion Hamilton in her Shaughnessy Heights home, they assumed it was death by natural causes. She was a sixty-eight-year-old widow suffering from dementia who had lived in the rambling old house since the death of her elderly mother nine months before.

Hamilton had two guardians, both cousins, appointed to look after her. Olga Young had wanted to put Hamilton into a nursing home where she would receive around the clock attention; but Elouise Roads Wilson, Hamilton's co-guardian, told Young that she didn't want the estate to be "depleted" by the cost of private care. So Wilson left her law practice in Victoria and moved into **1491 Nanton Street** to take care of her cousin.

Police came to the house after Wilson called to report Hamilton's death. They found Hamilton lying behind the door of the room where she slept. There was no forced entry and nothing stolen.

It wasn't until George Shoebotham, the chief coroner's technician, examined the body at the city morgue that police decided to take a closer look. Shoebotham found spotted ligature marks around her neck. Either someone had strangled her, or she'd hanged herself with a thin cord or wire.

Hamilton was wearing a gold chain necklace and police at first took it for the cause of death. Later they found a length of nylon string under a chair in the room. After discovering that Wilson was the sole beneficiary of Hamilton's estate and the only person alone with her at the time of her death, they believed that rather than taking care of her cousin, she was actually looking after her future inheritance. The prosecution thought she'd got tired of waiting.

Police arrested Wilson on January 16, 1976 in Victoria and charged her with murdering her cousin.

Eunice Coote, Hamilton's ninety-three-year-old mother, had died in the same house in March 1975. Apparently, she was dead for two weeks, lying in the same bed and decomposing, all the while Hamilton trying to feed and care for her. In Wilson's defence, her lawyer posited that Hamilton may have killed her mother and later killed herself by looping the twine around her neck and tying the end to the handle of her bedroom door. But when the coroner exhumed Coote's body, they discovered the cause of death was not murder. The elder Coote had died from a heart condition.

Eunice and John Coote bought the Nanton Street house in the 1950s after Coote retired from a successful real-estate business. John Coote, Marion's father, died in 1964 aged eighty-three.

Wilson, the forty-seven-year-old lawyer from Victoria was the star witness. She told the jury that she became co-guardian after the death of Hamilton's mother the previous March in the same Shaughnessy house. She also admitted that she was the sole beneficiary to Hamilton's $175,000 estate. Wilson told the jury that Hamilton had told her she wanted to join her dead mother. Wilson said she often locked her cousin in her room to stop her wandering around the streets at night. On the night she died, she told the court that she and her husband Philip put Hamilton to bed around 7:00 P.M., and Philip took the bus to Victoria where he worked.

As a well-respected lawyer who practiced in Victoria, it seemed odd that she would risk murdering her cousin for a $175,000 inheritance. But then, it seemed even odder that she would leave her practice, her home, and her husband to take care of Hamilton. The police were also surprised that she didn't break a window to cover up the murder as a botched robbery, or that she left the string—the murder weapon—in the room.

Wilson's defence at one point tried to implicate Wilson's husband, arguing that strangulation was more of a male act; but the jury didn't buy it, and found her guilty of second-degree murder.

Chapter 10

GHOSTLY GATHERINGS

In 1966, Hetty Fredrickson got her fifteen minutes of fame when she mentioned to a reporter from a Chilliwack weekly that she and husband Douglas were sharing their twelve-room house with a couple of ghosts. A presence, says Fredrickson, was pulling open drawers and shifting an old iron bedstead in an upstairs room in the former Chilliwack boarding house on Williams Street. She started having nightmares about a terrified woman in a red dress with yellow flowers and saw a shape of a figure in the upstairs bedroom. She decided to paint the ghosts.

"It was not easy," she told a *Vancouver Sun* reporter. "Every time I tried to paint, the face would start out as a man even as I tried to paint a woman. But I really concentrated and at last painted a likeness of the woman."

Neighbours told her that a man committed suicide in the house in the 1950s. Someone else said a woman was murdered in the house and then cemented in its chimney.

But scarier than the changing painting and the rumoured deaths, was the public reaction. One Sunday, seven hundred people turned up at the Fredricksons to try to catch a glimpse of the Fredrickson's ghosts. They broke the front steps, prompting the couple to put up a "no sightseers" sign.

Whether you believe in them or not, it's hard not to enjoy a good ghost story. Resident ghosts are particularly interesting, and they come in all sorts of forms. Reports abound of hearing footsteps when no one else is in the house. Some feel a presence and others see an outline of a ghost. Sometimes the ghost is mischievous and hides things from the householders. Ghosts supposedly slam doors, fiddle with electrical appliances, and try to communicate with the living. Sometimes the ghost is a benign presence, and at other times, it's downright malevolent. While some homeowners proudly boast about their ghosts, others live in fear that it will affect the resale value of their home. Not surprisingly, ghosts do not discriminate where or whom they haunt.

CEPERLEY HOUSE, BURNABY

On December 15, 1985 *Province* reporter Damian Inwood wrote, "I awoke with a jolt, I felt that something had nudged my subconscious, trying to attract my attention, and I was suddenly afraid. A chilling presence seemed to be pushing its way into the room and filling it. I tried to scream but couldn't. I struggled to sit up, but seemed unable to move. I turned my head and tried to reach my partner, *Province* photographer Les Bazso, but he was fast asleep. Then as suddenly as it had arrived the Presence was gone. The room seemed warmer and I lay panting with relief in my sleeping bag."

It seems that to believe in ghosts, people must also be able to see them. The ghosts of Ceperley House, now the Burnaby Art Gallery, are more than obliging. Ceperley House is a huge Arts and Crafts house built near Deer Lake. The house is painted dark brown, and the leaded windows are foreboding on a winter day. And, like any good haunted house, this one has a history.

Grace Dixon married Henry Tracey Ceperley in 1894 in Vancouver. It was the first marriage for Grace, thirty-one, and the second for Henry, forty-three. At the time of the 1901 Census, the household consisted of Henry, Grace, seventeen-year-old daughter Ethelwyn, fifteen-year-old son Arthur, and the domestic, twenty-nine-year-old Effie Reiach.

Henry ran a successful real-estate and insurance business, but it was Grace who bought the land in 1909 and built the retirement house from money she'd inherited from her brother-in-law, A.G. Ferguson (the same Ferguson of Ferguson Point in Stanley Park). The proviso was that after her death, the money would go to the improvement of Stanley Park.

Grace named the estate Fairacres. In 1911, when the house was finished, it was the largest in Burnaby. A story in the local newspaper described it as a palatial home, "[Fairacres], with its fine lawns, terraces, rockeries, greenhouses, pumping station for irrigation, lodge stables and outbuildings, costing $150,000 is alone worth a visit to Deer Park. The estate comprises twenty acres, ten of which are landscaped."

Aside from the house, the only other buildings that remain are the stables, root house, steam plant, and chauffeur's cottage. A story printed on a plaque outside the cottage says,

FAIRACRES, ALSO KNOWN AS CEPERLEY HOUSE AND NOW AS THE BURNABY ART GALLERY. CIRCA, 1911.
PHOTO COURTESY OF JIM WOLF, CITY OF BURNABY.

"Mr. Muttit, the chauffeur, refused to move his family in. He was a fairly new arrival from England and a socialist who did not want to live a "feudal life" on the estate. He built a house on nearby Sperling Avenue."

The Ceperleys lived at the estate during summer and wintered in Vancouver. When Grace died in November 1917, the stipulation in her will was that Henry could keep Fairacres until his death, at which time money from the sale of the estate would fund a children's playground in Stanley Park.

After her death, Henry packed up, headed for the Vancouver Club, and leased out the Deer Park estate. In 1922, Fairacres sold to businessman and former Mayor of Vancouver Frederick Buscombe. After all expenses, Grace left a $13,000 legacy and detailed instructions for one of the nicest and largest playgrounds in Canada. Not much, if anything remains of the original playground, but at one time children threw themselves down giant slides and climbed on ladders and seesaws. Little ones played in the sandbox or cooled off in the wading pool, while older kids played tetherball, basketball and vol-

Grace Ceperley, Outside Fairacres, Circa, 1911.
Photo Courtesy of Jim Wolf, City of Burnaby.

leyball or practiced long jump or high jump. Ceperley Park, named in Grace's honour, sits next to the pool at Second Beach in Stanley Park.

Fairacres changed hands again in the mid-'30s and in 1939 sold to a group of Benedictine monks from Mount Angel, Oregon. The monks made some changes, took down the aviary, added a gym (now the James Cowan Theatre), and lived there for the next fifteen years. In 1954, they moved out to Westminster Abbey in Mission and sold the mansion to the Temple of the More Abundant Life.

The Temple was actually a thinly disguised cult, around which rumours swirled. Rumour has it that male teachers had to wear beards because facial hair acted as an antenna, allowing them to pick up vibrations emitted by the universe. In 1959, the cult was outed when a *Vancouver Sun* reporter wrote that its leader, Archbishop John, was a convicted bigamist with a string of extortion and wife-beating charges in the U.S., and a wall full of bogus degrees. Archbishop John eventually fled back to the U.S., and the City of Burnaby bought the estate in 1966. For a couple of years, Fairacres rented to Simon Fraser University students.

A whole host of characters could theoretically haunt the halls of Ceperley House: Grace, a politician, the monks, cult members, and frat-house students from the radical '60s.

Tally up the reported sightings, and Grace comes out on top. She appears to have a decent wardrobe because eye-witness accounts have her floating upstairs or walking around the gallery wearing flowing dresses in white, blue, or grey. A few have spotted her face in an upstairs window. In October 2000, a private security guard hired for a film shoot told a reporter from *Burnaby Now,* "When I saw that face in the window, I just about died," he said, indicating a set of glass panes on the second floor. "Sweet Jesus, I just looked up and there she was, looking down at me like I was doing something wrong. Then she disappeared, just like that."

Staff members say they've heard footsteps and windows opening and shutting on the top floor when no one is there—at least no one from this world.

Others say they've heard a rustling of satin, felt a chill, and smelt perfume or cigar smoke. Staff report missing keys, appliances that go off for no reason, calls that come in on a dead phone line, and a sprinkler system that turns itself on when the house and grounds get too crowded. One woman said she felt a hand grab her ankle as she went upstairs. Grace is the most popular sighting; but there are others. The poltergeist that lives in the basement has a penchant for moving tools around in the air and rearranging them in different spots. A staffer reported the apparition of a praying monk, who was apparently equally frightened or annoyed, because he got up, turned around and disappeared. The politician has not appeared in any of the reported sightings, although it's always possible that he's the cigar smoker.

OSBORNE ROAD, NORTH VANCOUVER

When Jennifer, Patrick, and their two young boys, Graham, then six, and three-year-old Angus moved into their Craftsman style bungalow in 1998, they didn't realize they'd be sharing their Upper Lonsdale house with strangers. But to Jennifer, an interior designer, it soon became obvious that they weren't alone.

"We really had some very unusual experiences when we first moved in," she says. "We even contacted the previous owners to ask if they'd had any strange experiences and they said 'no, no, no, there was nothing, it's fine we never had anything unusual happen.'" But things did happen. And they weren't easy to explain.

The boys each had their own room on the main floor of the house. "It made me a little anxious because they had always slept above us in the previous house," says Jennifer. "I was hyper aware of listening for them. There was one morning, it was very early, around 4:30 A.M. and I could hear running in the hallway downstairs. I jumped out of bed and came downstairs and both the boys were fast asleep. The next day at the same time, I found my youngest outside on the driveway. There's no way he could have unlocked the door. The next day he woke up, came upstairs and said, 'I can't sleep downstairs anymore because the boy and the girl are keeping me awake all night.'"

And other strange things happened. Jennifer had taken photos of the house when it first went up for sale. She says when they went back some time later to look at the photos, they could see a little face gazing out from the window that was now Angus' room.

"All of those things were unusual, but they could have explanations other than there was a ghost in the house; but at the time, there were a lot of things," she says. "Doors were opening and closing—never when I could see them, but I could always hear them."

City directories show the house as "new" in 1925. The first owners were William Gilbert, a compositor for *The Vancouver Sun,* and his wife Nellie. They lived there until 1948. The next owners lived in the house for fifteen years.

Four years before Jennifer and Patrick bought the house in 1994, *The North Shore News* published an article with a sketch of the house and the headline, "A ghostly past may still haunt heritage house." Columnist Dorothy Foster wrote, "The present owner told me an interesting story about her house. One day she was working in the garden when a woman drove up and told her that they had previously lived in the house and that two 'entities' lived in that home as well. The woman went on to describe the first entity as a lovely young woman and the other ghostly figure as an angry old man."

Another time, a friend came to visit. While the owner was making tea, she saw the friend run out of the house, jump into her car and drive off. Later she told the owner that she'd seen a vision of a pretty young woman dressed in black in the living room, and upon going upstairs, she was confronted by the apparition of an angry old man."

Jennifer wasn't able to find any explanation for her ghost when she researched the past owners, but she's sure that it was two children. After a few months everything stopped and she figures that the move disturbed the presence somehow. "It was all kind of bizarre."

TOWNSEND PLACE, NEW WESTMINSTER

It's possible that all the activity generated by people moving in and out of the Osborne Road house unsettled whatever presence lurked there. For current owners Jim and Lou, a massive renovation of their Townsend Place house in New Westminster may have awoken the ghosts.

Whatever the reason, for a few years, the old house was haunted. Jim and Lou moved into the thirteen-room house in 1967. At that time, it was sixty-one-years-old and, like an elderly person, came with a history. As Jim said, the house had also "taken a hell of a beating over the years." As a carpenter, he was able to begin a major renovation.

The haunting started casually enough. About two years after Jim and Lou moved in, the downstairs tenant asked them about a "medicine smell." Jim and Lou had noticed the same old ointment kind of smell, and thought it was something that the tenant was using. And, sometimes, a light switch with a tricky control would switch on and off.

Once, an old family friend was staying overnight. "He woke up and saw a man looking out the window and the guy disappeared when he got out of bed," says Jim. "The dog was under the bed and wouldn't come out." The friend described a middle-aged man wearing a long coat and hat that looked like it came from a very different generation.

Before she died in 1988, Lou had a number of encounters. She would often feel a presence that she described to a *Vancouver Sun* reporter in 1982 as "a whirlwind around me. It's cold and follows me." She once saw an outline of a woman in a long dress and often talked of a presence that sat near her on the couch. The family dog, Rags, frequently stared at something that wasn't there.

Jim and Lou had three boys who shared the same bedroom. One night David, who was about ten at the time, called his mother into his room in the middle of the night. "He told her the coat hangers were floating," says Jim. "His two brothers were in the same room asleep, and he swore up and down that the coat hangers were floating."

Jim has had two unsettling experiences.

Several years after moving into the house, he was going upstairs to bed. He turned out the lights downstairs, and when he got to the foot of the staircase he reached out for the newel post. Someone or something grabbed his hand and continued to hold it as he went up the stairs. He wasn't scared, but it was strange, and he had to shake his hand free.

Jim's only other experience happened shortly after Lou died in 1988. One night after he'd gone to bed, he woke to see a white smoky shape near his head. The shape gave off a faint glow.

Interestingly, he says at no time did the family ever feel threatened by the activity. "No, there was never anything that made me worry," he says. "That experience was quite dramatic, I guess you'd say. It scared me at first."

Jim, a pragmatic sort of guy, is not entirely comfortable with the notion of ghosts. Does he believe in them? "I have no reason not to. There could be an explanation or not," he says. "A psychic came through here once and said, no there are no ghosts here now. But he said it's like when you live in a house or in a neighbourhood for a long time and then one day someone comes by to visit. So they come and they go."

Sounds like the psychic was right: Jim still lives in the house and the last time anything odd happened was in 1989.

PREMIER STREET, NORTH VANCOUVER

Another North Vancouver ghost that made front page news, this time in the 1970s, lived on Premier Street. At the time, single Mom Avril MacIntyre, twenty-one, and Jason, her three-and-a-half-year-old son, lived in a second floor unit.

Avril told a *Province* reporter that the haunting started when her son was very young. "I found him one night sitting up in bed roaring with laughter," she said. "As he grew older, the number of experiences grew. When he was two, I went into his bedroom one night and it was in chaos. Bedding was ripped, toys smashed, and the legs of his bed had been torn off. I had heard no noises prior to entering his room."

Jason dubbed the ghost "Johnny," and for some time Avril thought it was her son's imaginary friend. Avril's apartment is one of dozens built along the road near Capilano College. The Burrard Indian Band said the land was once the site of their ancient burial ground and claimed the ghost as their own.

Avril listed off some other weird happenings. A blender flew off a shelf, travelled several feet in the air, and fell on the floor. Another time, cupboard doors and drawers flew open. An ornamental bottle flew off a table and hit the couch. Neighbours talked of pictures that moved, growling noises (no dog), spinning lamps, and a vase that filled itself with water.

When Jason was old enough to talk, he described "Johnny" as over six feet tall with fair hair and dressed in buckskins—a bit like television favourite Daniel Boone. Avril would hear Jason talking to Johnny at 4:00 A.M., and an adult voice speaking back.

Avril bought a Ouija board and tried a séance one night to learn more about her house guest. After a piece moved without human intervention, she called a Catholic priest. "He told me to burn the board," she told *Province* reporter Philip Mills at the time. "We needed two cans of fuel in the end, the board just wouldn't burn."

Next came the psychics. One told Avril that she felt "eerie" while they swished cedar branches around the apartment. Her conclusion? "Indians just don't like white men building on their burial grounds." Not to be outdone, a psychologist specializing in psychic phenomena concluded that it was actually Jason behind all the weird stuff with his gift of psycho kinesis—the ability to move objects around just by thinking about them. Jason, according to the theory, was empowered with this "gift" after his father (tall with fair hair) left when he was a baby.

After 1976, Avril's name disappears from the city directories. She probably got as far away as she could, both from Johnny and the media circus that followed.

THE MOLE HILL GHOSTS

In the 1960s, the City of Vancouver started buying up houses along Comox Street in the West End with the intent to eventually bulldoze them and double the size of Nelson Park. Sitting just behind St. Paul's Hospital, in the area known as Mole Hill, the houses are a mix of mostly Queen Anne and Edwardian and stretch in a square around Comox, Thurlow, Bute and Pendrell Streets.

If the idea of demolition wasn't enough to rattle a few ghosts, one of the living residents, Blair Petrie, set about spearheading a five-year campaign to save the houses. He carefully researched the past owners of the houses and wrote a book about the area published in 1995. As part of his research, he made a couple of ghostly discoveries.

The residents of a house on Thurlow Street were convinced they had a female ghost. The house was one of four built in 1903 by a doctor who went into real-estate speculation, the favourite sideline of almost anyone with a few bucks at the time. He most likely flipped it straight away, after which it changed hands over the years to a number of different, mostly working class people. When Petrie started his research, the house was a bed and breakfast. The two young guys who ran the B&B would find a light turned on after they had turned it off, and once found a room locked from the inside. Most convincing were the actual sightings. "They had both witnessed this ghost and had many of their customers over the years come down to breakfast totally freaked out," says Petrie.

The ghost only showed herself in one bedroom and always wore a high-necked night-dress. The bed and breakfast proprietors found old markings on the floor, and figured out where the original furniture once sat. From the placing, they could imagine her brushing her long blonde hair in front of the dresser mirror.

Most of the sightings were by women who generally chose to stay in that particular room. Evidently she was a polite ghost, because she spoke to two of the guests and asked one of them, "Are you being taken care of here?"

Petrie couldn't find anything in the house's history to explain the ghost. Now that the house has changed owners and has been stripped to its studs and remodelled into rental suites, he says he doesn't know whether the ghost stayed or moved somewhere more accommodating.

Apparently she's not the only Mole Hill ghost. In the 1990s, the City of Vancouver finally agreed to keep and renovate twenty-seven of these heritage houses and engaged two architectural firms to do the work. Petrie was in a Comox Street house with two architects there to photograph and catalogue the heritage details and work out how they would preserve them. "We went upstairs and this one architect stayed downstairs. We came walking back down fifteen minutes later and he was standing at the foot of the stairs literally white as a ghost, and he said he had seen a ghost," says Petrie. "He said he was in this room taking photographs of door knobs and things, and all of a sudden he felt this chill and the door slammed. The room was in the interior of the house, and it wasn't windy. He swore it was a ghost, and it freaked him out. He said 'I'm not coming back here.' I'm not sure if he saw anything or not, but that's the closest I've come to witnessing a ghost in Mole Hill myself."

IRVING HOUSE

Irving House is a Gothic Revival overlooking the Fraser River and planted on what's now busy Royal Avenue. The whole house feels spooky. The wallpaper and the carpets in the two front parlours are original, the bed where Irving died is still there and the furniture, the clothes, and the gadgets are all authentic to the period. The house hasn't left the 1860s and it feels like the family has just stepped out for a moment.

Irving went to sea as a cabin boy at age fifteen and worked his way up the ranks. When he hit Oregon, he left the ocean for riverboats, married Elizabeth Dixon of Portland and by 1858 settled in New Westminster. Called the "King of the River," by the early 1860s the Scottish born Irving had considerable clout. He had the family home built from boat-loads of redwood shipped up from California. The newspaper called it "the handsomest, the best and most home-like house of which British Columbia can yet boast."

Irving died in 1872, and Elizabeth eventually returned to Oregon. John Irving took over his dad's company at age seventeen and turned out to be a formidable businessman. In 1883, he formed the Canadian Pacific Navigation Company and sold it in 1901 to Canadian Pacific Limited. John's sister Mary married Thomas Briggs and they raised nine children at Irving House, which they called Hollymount. Two of the unmarried daughters Naomi and Manuela lived in the house until 1950 when it was sold to the City for five thousand dollars.

After the City bought Irving House, Betty Miller, the mother of Archie Miller, a former curator, had a few strange experiences when staying at the house. On one anniversary of the death of Captain Irving, she felt his ghost brush past her on the stairs saying, "I must make haste." Another time, a small boy about eight years old with a school tour refused to come into the house. He simply said, "I can't come in." Once a woman who came to visit the house, entered the front parlour and said "I'm sorry, I can't stay," before she fled.

Jim Wolf, a heritage planner with the City of Burnaby, is a believer. He's heard a dozen ghost stories about Irving House; he's even experienced one himself.

"When I first worked there it was almost electric," he says. "The house definitely has a lot of energy."

Wolf started researching the history of Irving House in the 1980s. He said the only time he felt uneasy was one morning when he was working in John Irving's old bedroom. "I'm sitting down cross-legged on the floor doing some cataloguing, and my body literally froze up. I knew there was something behind me and that if I turned around I was

IRVING HOUSE, CIRCA 1880.
PHOTOGRAPHER UNKNOWN.
COURTESY OF THE NEW WESTMINSTER PUBLIC LIBRARY, PHOTO # 254.

going to see it. I put my pen down and with all of my might I made my body move out of that room, and I never looked back. It was the creepiest feeling I've ever had in that house."

The ghost stories about Irving House go back to its beginnings as a public building. For security reasons, a curator and caretaker—usually a married couple—lived in a basement suite in the house. In the 1960s, Albert Walker was curator and his wife Queenie led the tours. It was her job to prepare the house for visitors. One morning, her small grand-daughter was visiting and helping Queenie prepare the upstairs bedroom. The little girl came skipping down the hallway and told her grandmother that there was a man on the bed in John's room. Queenie went into the room, saw that the bed's antique coverlets were all twisted, and told her granddaughter not to play on the bed ever again. The next morning, the same thing happened. This time she knew the little girl wasn't in the room. "Look, there he is again," she told her grandmother. And as Queenie turned she saw the twisted blankets exactly as if an adult was asleep in the bed.

A few years later, one of the guides regularly opened up the house to an overpowering smell of lilacs. One day after the last visitors had gone through the house, she was getting ready to lock up when she heard footsteps on the second floor. She called, "Hello, is anybody there. Hello!" Nobody answered, but she kept hearing the footsteps, felt more and more uneasy, and called for another staff member to come up and help. As her colleague was going up the stairs, he moved aside for somebody who was coming down. He stopped and said, "Oh, excuse me," as something shoved up against him. But there was never anybody else on those stairs.

Wolf says that another time when he was in the house, a patient came over from nearby St. Mary's hospital and asked him if children lived there. "I asked her why, and she said she was looking out of her window at the hospital the night before, and there were three little girls dancing on the lawn in their white nightgowns."

One Christmas the museum manager and a volunteer were putting red baubles on a tree in an upstairs bedroom. All of a sudden, the volunteer announced that he had to go and quickly disappeared, leaving the manager alone in the room. A short time later, the manager started to feel strange and walked out of the room. As she turned to look back, she saw that a red bauble had rolled out of the parlour and was rolling down the hallway toward her, moved by some unseen force.

Another time, a caretaker had a friend stay in the house while he went away for the weekend. Wolf tells the story: "He's in the house and he hears footsteps on what he thinks is one of the outside porches. So he marches out armed with a flashlight ready to take on anybody who is prowling around the house in the middle of the night," he says. "As he's going by the library window he sees a small blue light that looks like a blue orb floating in the middle of the room. It starts to spin and it rushes toward the window and when it gets to the window he sees a person's face, slam up against the glass. He is so freaked out that he doubles back and falls eight feet onto the ground and keeps running."

Chapter 11

EAST MEETS WEST

B̲ob Rennie, Vancouver's Condo King, walked into the bowels of the building at **51 East Pender Street** and stood outside a boarded up door. He lifted the top bar easily, but had a bit more trouble with the bottom one. Looking around, he found a shovel to lever it off and yanked the door open. He then rolled up his expensive shirt sleeves and climbed up the six flights of stairs, past rat traps, broken windows, and old stoves.

Rennie paid one million dollars for the Wing Sang building, the oldest building in Chinatown. And that was just for the battered walls, the shaky staircase, and a hundred-plus years of history. He bought it sight unseen in 2004 and didn't go inside for the first six months.

Built in 1889, and long abandoned, the Wing Sang building is now the headquarters of Rennie Marketing Systems. When Rennie eventually saw the building, he decided that rebuilt and restored, the former living quarters of Yip Sang's huge family would make ideal offices. The twenty-seven thousand square foot space with the soaring ceilings would also be perfect for his own private "art space" to house his collection of work by contemporary artists like Richard Prince and Brian Jungen. The building butts up against this century's development of twenty-two "Chinatown flats" with the Rennie marketing slogan, "A Cultural Property."

"People think I'm crazy," he said. "It will probably bankrupt me."

What a difference a century or so makes.

Back in 1889, the population of Vancouver was around fifteen thousand. The core of the city was Gastown, and Pender Street was still Dupont Street. Chinatown was a fledgling community where most of the Chinese population lived, and Chinatown merchants rented most of the buildings.

Members of the Yip Sang Family in Front of the Wing Sang Building, Circa 1901. Courtesy of Henry Yip.

Then came Yip Sang. Born in 1845 in the Shengtang Village, Guangdong province in southern China, he came to Vancouver in the 1880s via Hong Kong, San Francisco, and the Yukon. After working at everything from cigar-making to cooking and dishwashing, he became the agent for the Canadian Pacific Railway. Yip Sang hired the Chinese workers and soon became a leader among the Chinese.

Yip Sang built the original two-storey Victorian Italianate structure to house his growing import/export business, the Wing Sang Company. He operated an informal bank and travel agency, through which Chinese workers could send money to relatives in China and book passage on steamships home. The Wing Sang Company sold everything from Chinese silks and curios to opium, at least until it was made illegal in 1908. As the business grew, so did the building.

The Wing Sang building is actually a couple of buildings. In 1901, Yip Sang added a third storey with bay windows and extended the building, adding more shops at the retail level. In 1912, he built a six-storey building, across the alley behind Pender and connected by an elevated passageway, to include a warehouse, a meeting place, and a floor for each of his three wives and their twenty-three children.

He housed struggling Chinese immigrants on the first floors of the building until they could get work in Canada.

Henry Yip was born in 1917 on the fourth floor of the building. He was only ten when his grandfather died, but as the son of Kew Mow, number three son of first wife, he remembers Yip Sang as a "disciplinarian."

"He was very tough on the family," says Henry Yip. "He used to sit beside a potbelly stove next to the doorway at the front of the building smoking his pipe and watching everybody go in and out." Yip Sang had a strict curfew, and as the only one with a key, would lock out family members still not home by 10:00 P.M. "He would say, you people are in or you are out," recalls Henry Yip.

Henry Yip says that while Yip Sang was tough on the family, he was also very generous. He remembers three large woks in the back of the building continuously cooking food for the family and the new immigrants from China, and to take to the Chinese Benevolent Association, which he founded.

Sang also built a seven-storey building in Shanghai Alley to house new immigrants, as well as the first Chinese school and hospital. He eventually had several businesses, including a hotel and three canneries. He was the first to export salted fish to China, a venture that grew into a huge business.

Walking into the part of the building that fronts onto Pender Street, and the part Rennie will save, feels like stepping back into the nineteenth century. The original wainscoting is still on the walls of the schoolroom where Henry Yip and his many cousins used to study Chinese on the weekends. This room is now Rennie's corporate boardroom.

At a time when racism was rampant, Yip Sang pushed all his kids—nineteen sons and four daughters—to get an education. One son, Ghim, was Canada's first Chinese medical doctor, another, seventeenth son Dock, was the first Chinese person called to the bar. Dock's daughter graduated from New York's Columbia University and was the first woman to teach at the Vancouver Chinese Overseas School. Quene, sixteenth son, was a star centre forward soccer player.

In those days, when Chinese could not vote, and faced daily ridicule, anti-Chinese movements, political hatred, and dangerous labour conditions, the boys from the Yip, the Louie, the Cumyow, and other Chinese pioneer families courageously formed a soccer team. During the 1920s and 30s, it was the only Chinese-Canadian soccer team in the country. When they played, Chinatown closed down to watch. It was one of the few things that put the Chinese on an equal footing with the rest of the country, and their players were heroes.

In 1933, the team won the B.C. Mainland Cup, defeating all other senior soccer teams in the province. Henry Yip remembers the next day as a holiday in Chinatown with free tea and dim sum.

As well as being a star soccer player on the first soccer team at the University of British Columbia, Quene Yip was also a track star. Born in 1905, he became a chemist, a writer, and a translator. He lived until the age of eighty-eight.

The commercial area of the Wing Sang building lined Pender Street, and Chinese shops, services and restaurants changed hands frequently. One of the longest and best known tenants was the landmark B.C. Royal Café. The café operated from 1925 to 1965 and is featured in Denise Chong's book, *The Concubine's Children.*

Yip Sang died in 1927, but his family ran the Wing Sang Co. until 1989. His more than six hundred descendants, now spread over five generations, sold the forty thousand square foot building in 2001.

The Chinese have shown amazing resilience throughout their history in British Columbia. Paid a pittance for their work compared to their white counterparts, the Chinese workers were given the most difficult and dangerous jobs and then derided for taking less money. The government passed laws to stop Chinese laundries and restaurants from hiring white women and provincial capital projects from employing Chinese.

More than six hundred Chinese workers died building the railroad, and when it was finished, the Canadian government slapped a head tax of fifty dollars on further immigration. The head tax increased to one hundred dollars in 1900. A Royal Commission found that Chinese were "obnoxious to a free community and dangerous to the state," and in 1903, the federal government increased the head tax to five hundred dollars effectively wiping out all Chinese immigration until 1908. In 1923, the government introduced the Chinese Immigration Act that virtually eliminated all migration from China until 1947. No Chinese women immigrated during this time, leaving the Chinese population as a lonely bachelor society. The only exceptions to the Act were teachers, church personnel, and consular staff.

THOMAS MOORE WHAUN

In 1907, Tung Mow Wong spent twenty-six days on a ship from China, survived a robbery on board, and arrived in Vancouver thirteen-years-old and dead broke. He would have found Vancouver, or what the Chinese called "Gold Mountain," bewildering. At that time,

racism was at its height. The Asiatic Exclusion League formed that year to lobby the government to stop Asian immigration. The group burned effigies and carried signs saying
"stop the yellow peril," and "keep Canada white." That September, a riot of white workers
protesting cheap Chinese labour trashed Chinatown.

Wong, who anglicized his name to Thomas Moore Whaun, managed to get a job as
a house boy for a white family where he picked up some English. He saved what he
could, all the while dreaming of an education. In 1921 he enrolled at the University of
British Columbia. While his compatriots were working in sawmills and restaurants,
Whaun learned about the French Revolution. He read the poetry of Shelley, Keats, and
Byron, and the classics of Plato, Kant and Confucius, majoring in economics and
political science. He was also a member of the International Club of Vancouver, which
hosted guest lecturers such as Bertrand Russell and Pearl S. Buck.

Whaun's daughter, Dr. June Whaun, says other Chinese could not understand why he
would waste his time studying. "They couldn't understand why he was going to university,
especially a white man's university," she says. "They thought he was a freak of nature."

Whaun took two years away from his studies to run a grocery store in Point Grey and
save to finish his education. When he graduated in 1927, he was one of the first Chinese-
Canadians to earn a degree. His classmates included Dal Grauer, who would eventually
run B.C. Electric, and future ad man Jimmy Lovick.

It was while Whaun was at U.B.C. that the Canadian government introduced the
Chinese Exclusion Act in 1923. That year, he led a nation-wide letter writing campaign to one hundred English daily newspapers across Canada protesting this senseless
discrimination. Whaun's letter writing campaigns to politicians and others he called
"big wigs" continued throughout his life, and, in later decades, he corresponded with
people such as John Diefenbaker, Hugh Keenleyside, and Douglas Jung. Copies of the
letters, attached to news clippings, photos, and diaries can be seen at U.B.C.'s Special
Collections Archives.

The campaign resulted in a job offer from the *Canada Morning News*, one of two
Chinese daily newspapers operating in Vancouver. Whaun became the paper's advertising
manager. "My father gathered a band of fellow classmates who went and solicited advertising
from the Canadian advertising agencies," says June Whaun. "When someone brought in
three dollars worth of ads, the fellow who brought it in got one dollar, my father got one
dollar and the publishing company got one dollar."

When the paper folded, Whaun spent the next forty years as the public relations and
advertising officer for the *New Republic Daily*. He retired in 1973.

Most of Vancouver's Chinese-Canadians stayed in Chinatown or the Strathcona area for decades after immigration halted in 1923. But in 1931, Whaun bought a summer cottage on Twenty-second Street in West Vancouver. He, his wife Diamond, and their three daughters June, Patricia, and Mayling were the first non-Caucasians to venture into that white enclave. June, the eldest daughter, was the first Asian child born at the Lions Gate Hospital.

At that time the only way to get to Vancouver from the North Shore was by a half-hour ferry ride that sailed from the foot of Carrall Street to Ambleside and Fourteenth Street in West Vancouver. "He was usually out of the house at 7:00 A.M. because he wanted to get the ferry," says June Whaun. His daily rounds included visiting the office on East Pender Street, seeing advertisers, dropping in to the brokerage house to check on stocks, and stopping off in Chinatown for groceries.

"My father focused on great books," she says. "When I said I was reading *Black Beauty*, he said 'what is the matter with your brain!'"

Dr. Whaun now lives in Maryland, and, from all accounts, she's had a remarkable career. She graduated from the U.B.C. School of Medicine in 1960 and during the 1970s, was director of the oncology program at the University of Calgary. In the 1980s, the Walter Reed Army Institute of Research in Washington, D.C. recruited her as a colonel in the U.S. army. She worked as a haematologist/scientist, initially doing malaria research using comparative biochemistry for drug development. In 2003, she went back to school to earn a Master's in Public Health at Columbia University. She now works as a medical advisor for a large research organization involved in clinical trials for cancer drugs.

The house on Twenty-second Street was next to the Pauline Johnson School, which all three daughters attended. The Whauns lived there until 1947 when they moved up the street a little to **2347 Mathers Avenue.**

Whaun lived in the Mathers Avenue house until he died in 1985 at the age of ninety—one.

Dr. Whaun says she learned from her father that you have to be able to adapt to changing circumstances. "You don't get anywhere; you don't get traction by staying in place. You have to change, you have to learn, you constantly must reinvent yourself," she says. "My father believed that you have to treat people the way you wish to be treated. He considered himself to be a humanist. He didn't believe in any particular religion. Mother and father cheerfully inculcated in each of us that there are consequences of every action, so you have to think through [things] to find out what the bottom line is, because if it doesn't sound right, don't do it."

Any racism the Whauns experienced growing up in white West Vancouver was subtle, says June Whaun. "Of course there is racism. It's British Columbia. It's white Anglo protestant," she says. "When I went to medical school we had a quota: ten percent Jews, ten percent Asians and ten percent female. If I was Jewish, I would have fulfilled three quotas."

TONG LOUIE

When Tong and Geraldine Louie, both educated and successful business people, moved to Point Grey in 1941, they met with an entirely different reception.

A delegation bearing eighty-three signatures urged instant steps against the "intrusion of the Oriental into desirable residential districts." The petition, started after the Louies bought the house at **5810 Highbury Street,** sparked off a staggering chain of events. On February 4, 1941, the headline of a story in the *Daily Province* was, "Ban Orientals from Better Residential Areas." The story covered a city council meeting, during which Alderman H.D. Wilson warned that Japanese and Chinese were filtering into the city's newest and best sections. City council, said the story, would appoint a special committee to draft a by-law preventing orientals from being either owners or tenants in other than their own recognized localities.

The delegation asked for lower tax assessments in the Highbury area because of the sale to a Chinese family and appealed for restrictions to prevent repetition of the occurrence. "This is only an indication of what will face the city in years to come," declared Alderman Wilson. "Orientals have purchased property in the Little Mountain subdivision, and a number are going into the new residential districts where their presence has the immediate effect of reducing values. They just won't comply with our standards. Real-estate values are falling. Where one oriental buys property, another follows."

The leader of the keep Highbury white group told council that property values would immediately plunge twenty percent. Another member said the "Chinaman" had offered to pay eight hundred dollars more than other bidders.

Wilson assured the white folk with oriental servants that they would be unaffected by the by-law. "Such persons would be ruled members of the white household in which they were employed," he said.

The Daily Province and *The Vancouver Sun* ran stories about the Point Grey bigots, but neither newspaper mentioned the Louies by name.

Ernest Perrault, author of *Tong: The Story of Tong Louie, Vancouver's Quiet Titan*, and a friend of Louie's, says that the decision of the newlyweds to buy a house in Point Grey was very brave. "In his own quiet way, he stirred a lot of things up. He had the guts to move into what was a one hundred percent white community and make a success of it. He stayed there and toughed it out," says Perrault. "Louie's attitude was, 'I am not going to be denigrated because I am Chinese. I am a capable human being, and whether they like it or not, I am going to function at the same level they function.'"

Perrault says a warm welcome by their next door neighbours helped sustain the Louies when they moved into the area, adding that "people who were his enemies became his reluctant friends, and some of them his very close warm friends."

Others wrote to the newspapers appalled by the racism. Under the heading "Oriental Ghettos," one letter said, "Decent minded Canadians will not permit 'pure Aryan' ideology to take root here. Events in Europe prove that Aryanism rapidly leads to pogroms and ghettos." Another asked, "Who is this Alderman Wilson? He appears to suffer from some personal spite against the Chinese and Japanese. The next move will be to place them in concentration camps. People are becoming disgusted with this anti-British attitude toward other Canadian citizens."

Unfortunately, it did little to slow Alderman Wilson. A notice in *The Vancouver Sun* a few months later advised readers that the Dunbar-West Point Grey Community Association was holding a meeting the following Monday, at which Alderman H.D. Wilson would speak on the "prevention of penetration of Orientals into Point Grey district."

The Louies stuck it out. They lived on Highbury Street until 1967 when they moved a few blocks to a larger house at Southlands Place.

Tong Louie was born in Vancouver in 1914. He was the second of eleven children born to Hok Yat (H.Y.) Louie, a Chinese immigrant who had come to Canada in 1896. Hok Yat taught himself English and, in the face of overwhelming racism and brutal competition, built a small general store that catered to Chinese farmers. With the help of his sons, he built this small store into a giant food empire in one of the toughest periods in Vancouver's history for the Chinese.

In the 1930s, Chinese people couldn't practice law, medicine, or pharmacology. They couldn't teach in public schools or work for the government. In this environment, Tong chose a degree in agriculture and graduated with a Bachelor of Science degree from U.B.C. in 1938. Like most Chinese families in the early years of the twentieth century, the Louies lived in Chinatown. At first they lived in cramped quarters above the store, but as business improved, Hok Yat built a two-storey brick building at **254 East Georgia Street** in 1930.

The Louie name is now a Vancouver institution. According to *Business in Vancouver*, The H.Y. Louie Company is the second largest private company in the province after the Jim Pattison Group. The family owns the IGA chain of supermarkets and local success story London Drugs, which is gradually making its way across the country. Tong Louie believed in giving back to the community, and before he died in 1998, he became a bene-factor to universities and non-profit organizations such as the Vancouver Public Library and the Vancouver Symphony Orchestra.

DESTRUCTION OF A NEIGHBOURHOOD

By the 1950s, Vancouver's population growth was so great that even though the Chinese moved away from Chinatown, the Chinese population in adjacent Strathcona steadily increased. Only a decade before, city council had tried to ghettoize the Chinese in Chinatown, and by 1959, the very existence of the Chinese community in Vancouver was threatened.

City planners declared Strathcona a slum slated for demolition. "Urban renewal"—a term that sounded like something out of a George Orwell novel—was the new buzz word, and one that would save the residents from themselves. As part of the city's urban renewal plan for Strathcona, the city froze property values in 1958 and from then on, stopped any regular public works maintenance in the area and stopped issuing any redevelopment or home improvement permits. Many of these Chinese home owners lived in extended fam-ilies and, although many couldn't speak English, they were quite self-sufficient. Urban renewal would see them stashed into soulless subsidized public housing.

According to a January 15, 1966 *Vancouver Sun* story, "The householder had three choices. He could move to another district; relocate within the area in an effort to keep one jump ahead of the house wreckers; or move into public housing paying twenty per-cent of the family income as rent. One owner who received $6,000 from the sale of his house pays $75 per month or $900 a year in rent. This includes heat and taxes, which cost about $250 a year so his increased housing expense is about $650 a year net." An equivalent house in a nearby neighbourhood sold for close to $20,000.

If accepted, the overall plan would displace nine thousand Chinese in a one hundred million dollar redevelopment program. It threatened to destroy Chinatown as residents reluctantly moved away from the area. The first phase, in 1969, saw thirty acres bulldozed to make way for the MacLean Park high-rise and the Raymur-Campbell Public Housing

Project. Three years later, the city's seventeen million dollar second phase went ahead, displacing twenty-three hundred people, mostly Chinese. By 1967, the city had cleared fifteen blocks of houses. Then the city announced its plan to construct a freeway between Union and Prior Streets. Connected via a new Georgia Viaduct, the freeway would carve up parts of Chinatown and Gastown.

This wholesale uprooting and demolition of the area continued until November 1968 when six hundred local residents founded the Strathcona Property and Tenants Association (SPOTA). Sue Lum, Walter Chan, and Harry Con became co-chairs of SPOTA.

HARRY CON

Harry Con was born on October 29, 1922 in Coquitlam. When he was quite young the family moved back to China returning to Canada in the mid 1930s, smack in the middle of the depression. His daughter, Ada Con, says, "When he came back, he was fourteen and went to Strathcona School." He was stuck in grade two because he couldn't speak English.

When the Chinese Freemasons started a Chinese school at Carrall and Pender, Con became principal. In 1957 he opened a store on East Pender and imported and sold Chinese curios. In 1963 he added a post office, the only one in Chinatown. "One thing about my father is that he was very community oriented and whatever he felt that the community had given to him, he wanted to give back," says Ada. "He was always at meetings and SPOTA would meet at our house."

Con always stood up for what he believed was right. At the age of twenty-two, he attended a meeting at the United Church at Dunlevy and Pender Streets to debate whether Chinese should join the army or ignore the call. "If we didn't, well, maybe the government would have the right to say, 'you guys didn't serve in the war, didn't answer the call, and you don't deserve it.' Maybe this discrimination would be permanent," Con said in *Opening Doors* in 1979. "So for that reason we voted to answer the government's call."

Con was one of about two hundred Chinese from British Columbia who served in South East Asia in Force 136, a secret service commando group that parachuted into Burma and Malaysia and specialized in sabotage and reconnaissance behind Japanese enemy lines. After the war finished in 1945, Con started work for the *Chinese Times* as a news translator. Two years later, the government repealed the exclusion act.

HARRY CON OUTSIDE HIS HOUSE, 1980s.
PHOTO COURTESY OF ADA CON.

In 1982, Harry Con was awarded the Order of Canada, and four years later he was named a Vancouver Pioneer of Distinction. Harry Con died in 1993, but his wife Lily stayed in the family home at **329 East Pender Street** that her father-in-law built in the 1930s. It's a sturdy three-storey home in Strathcona right on the edge of Chinatown. If not for the efforts of people like the Cons, that house, most of Strathcona, and a chunk of Chinatown and Gastown would now be sitting under a sea of concrete.

The house now sits on a twenty-five by 125 square foot lot next to a seniors' centre. Over the years, the Cons have added to it, and while there's nothing really architecturally significant about the house, its social history is an important part of the history of Strathcona.

MARY CHAN

Mary Chan also received a Vancouver Pioneer of Distinction award in 1986. And while her role was very different from Harry Con's, she was just as instrumental in saving Strathcona. Mary Chan almost single handedly drummed up the support and the energy to save her neighbourhood. Shirley Chan remembers accompanying her mother while she knocked on doors, talked, cajoled, and canvassed donations to hire a lawyer to take on City Hall. The Chans held early organizing meetings in their large Edwardian house at **658 Keefer Street**. Later the meetings moved between the Chan's house, the Con's house, the First United Church, Chinatown restaurants, and coffee shops.

Mary's grandfather, Lee Ying Yat, came to Canada in 1879 hoping to strike it rich in the gold rush. It didn't work out, and he started work on the railroad. He managed to save enough money to buy some boggy land along the waterfront, eventually expropriated for the Port of Vancouver for two hundred dollars. He used this money to bring his son Joe Lee to Canada, who married and had ten children. Mary was daughter number three.

The family struggled until 1923, and when the government announced the Chinese Immigration Act, they gave up and went back to China. Mary was eight. By the 1940s, China was an unstable place and Mary now married to Walter Chan, a teacher, and pregnant with Shirley, returned to Canada in 1947 after the Act was lifted. She worked three jobs, mostly in Gastown clothing factories, until she had enough money to bring her husband to Canada. They wanted to bring their children up close to Chinatown where they could learn to speak Chinese and retain the culture. By 1955, they'd saved enough money to buy the house on Keefer Street from the Minichiello family.

Soon after moving into their house, the Chans learned about the urban renewal program. Thinking that if they fixed up their house, they'd be able to keep it, they hired people to do repairs. Then they discovered that the entire neighbourhood would be demolished.

Now the Director of Sustainable Development for Health Canada, in 1968, Shirley Chan was a Simon Fraser University student studying for a bachelor's degree in English. "Mom had a natural organizing ability," she says.

CHAN FAMILY, OUTSIDE 658 KEEFER STREET (HOUSE ON THE RIGHT), CIRCA 1968.
FROM LEFT TO RIGHT, FRONT ROW: LARRY CHAN, GRANDMOTHER LIM HOP LEE, SHIRLEY CHAN
BACK ROW: MARY CHAN, KAREN CHAN (BABY) NICK LUM, WALTER CHAN,
PHOTO COURTESY OF SHIRLEY CHAN.

Shirley says she went door to door with her mother. "Whenever there was any issue that was important, Mom would drag me around after work or on weekends, and my job was to translate for her, except I never had to translate because she always did all the talking herself anyway. She was just afraid she might not understand something."

Shirley's brother Larry Chan says their mother was known as the "field marshal."

"She was a big strong woman willing to use physical force and manual labour to accomplish things, and she was the perfect opposite of my father, he being quiet and academically accomplished," he says. "In meetings, my mother would pound the table to get people's attention and then address everybody with a loud voice to make her point. My father would have people stop and ask him for his thoughts. They worked well together that way. It was very effective."

The women of SPOTA used food to lobby politicians. "We did a lot of things around food," says Shirley. "We organized tea parties and we had banquets. Whenever a cabinet minister came to town or somebody important we'd fundraise with these banquets."

In 1969, the planners at City Hall organized a tour for federal minister of housing Paul Hellyer. He invited Shirley to go with him on the bus. "I had an opportunity to show him these houses that were still true. Okay the porch might need to be replaced, but the fact is it was still decent, safe, affordable housing for these families." He returned to Ottawa and announced a freeze on urban renewal.

"It was a tremendous victory, and we used opportunities like this to bring the community together and know that we had achieved something special to have stopped urban renewal and changed national housing policy."

When Mike Harcourt was elected mayor in 1980, Shirley became his executive assistant and chief of staff.

Mary Chan died in December, 2002. "My mother was the one who really believed in an active democratic government where, as a citizen, you had the right and the power to go and make a difference. I miss her," she says.

Larry Chan, a successful Vancouver naturopathic doctor, now owns the three-storey family home. He applied for a heritage designation and his plan is to develop the property to stay true to its heritage qualities, live in part of the house, and sell some of it off to finance the renovation. "I believe that from a historic basis of urban planning and development in Vancouver, the house needs to be preserved," says Larry. "Personally, I would like my own children to realize the important role that my parents had in preserving Strathcona."

Chapter 12

RESEARCHING YOUR OWN HOME'S HISTORY

In some ways, researching your home is like undertaking an archaeological dig. There are tons of steps involved, you need lots of patience, but the rewards are immense. You can find out who built your home, who lived there before you, who was murdered there, who died of a comfortable old age, perhaps, even, who is haunting it now.

This might sound obvious, but take it from someone who works from a few dozen cards, a drawer full of files, and several boxes—get organized and write everything down: page numbers, dates, names, references. You might think you'll remember, but once you go back in time it will all start to blur.

DATING YOUR HOUSE

How to date your house? A simple question you'd think, but there's nothing simple about research. Sometimes, though, you can get lucky.

Contact City Hall and ask what they have on file for your address. With luck, the building permit or the water connection records will date your property. I found out that my house was actually two houses. The owner built the first storey on the lot and the second storey was a bungalow moved from a different site in the area. It explained, for instance, why there was no hardwood floor in the living room, but when we took out a rancid bedroom carpet we found a pristine oak floor with mahogany insets.

ARCHITECTURE

The style of your house also offers up some good research opportunities. It's worth picking up a good guide to architecture that will help you tell the difference between a finial, a barge-board, or a gable for instance. The Vancouver Heritage Foundation has a little booklet called

Your Old House, which you can download at vancouverheritagefoundation.org. This booklet gives you a sort of connect-the-dots guide to doodads and pictures, so you can tell the difference between the Queen Anne style, a more staid Edwardian Vernacular, or a neo-Classical. It dates the period they went up and, if nothing else, you'll sound extremely authoritative at dinner parties. The problem with Vancouver houses is most of them seem to be a mishmash of several styles, or the renovations over several decades have left them wearing a number of different features.

THE HERITAGE INVENTORY

The Vancouver Heritage Register lists over twenty-two hundred commercial and residential heritage buildings and historical landmarks in the city. The city evaluates each house for its architectural, historical, and social value and then grades them into A, B, or C categories. Listed doesn't mean protected; less than twenty percent are protected through designation. If your house falls into one of the designations, it's worth noting that the city offers some incentives to discourage bulldozing your old pipes and bad wiring. Sometimes, the city will relax zoning and development by-laws, allowing owners of heritage buildings to do a variety of things that would otherwise be against local by-laws. If your house meets certain criteria, you can apply to the Vancouver Heritage Foundation for a True Colours grant, which will help you bring your house back to its original heritage colours.

Most municipalities put out some form of heritage inventory, and some, such as New Westminster's, are even available on line. You can find others at your local library, archives, or City Hall. They usually give the address, the date, the architect, and a paragraph about the architecture. Sometimes they'll mention a prominent former resident or first owner.

VANCOUVER BUILDING REGISTER

While most of the buildings are commercial, there are a number of residential buildings on the register. If yours is one of them, the entries come with the type of information a house researcher can usually only dream of. And it's all available to you online through the Vancouver Public Library. Get onto the website at vpl.ca and from the main menu screen, choose the "Library Catalogue" tab, and then click on "Community Resources," at the top of the page. Next, click on the "Vancouver Building Register" tab. You have a couple of choices here, you can either plug in the name of the building, the name of the architect, or the street address. When I plug in Aberthau, for example, I find out that it's now the West Point Grey Community Centre at 4397 West Second Avenue. The entry shows that architect Samuel Maclure designed the house in 1913 and that it has a heritage building designation. James S. Rear was the first resident and lived there from 1911 to 1918. In 1919, Colonel Victor Spencer bought the property, and in 1939, it became an RCAF officers' mess until 1968. From 1972 to the present time, it has operated as a community centre. The entry for Aberthau also tells me that address may have been 4395 West Second at one time, and that it has three storeys. And it also gives me several newspaper and magazine citations that I can look up at the library to find out more information about the house.

New Westminster

The New Westminster Museum and Archives has a building file that offers up the construction date and history, water connection dates, architectural style, site information, occupancy, business, and personal connections of various buildings and homes within the city. It's based on the heritage resource inventory and expanded by staff, so it's constantly evolving to include more information. The goal is to have a file of information for every building in the city.

Heritage House Tours

In 2003, the Vancouver Heritage Foundation started a house tour and, conveniently, they've posted every guidebook since then on their website. The books give historical descriptions of the different neighbourhoods, and each one has ten houses that range from modest Strathcona houses to massive Shaughnessy Heights mansions. While the focus is on the architecture, there is usually a nod to the social history of the houses. Go to vancouverheritagefoundation.org and click on the "Projects and Events" tab. Then click on "Open Vancouver Heritage House Tour." Scroll down to find the guidebooks.

If you live in New Westminster, you are really in luck. The New Westminster Preservation Society started doing house tours in 1980 and posted every guidebook on the website. Go to nwheritage.org and click on "Heritage Buildings." Then click on "Heritage Home Tours Database." Search by the name of the house, owner, architect, builder, address, or date of construction. You'll see an image of the house and a fairly lengthy detailed architectural and social history.

Getting Your Legal Description

A legal description is helpful for further research. You can find it on your property deed or on the property assessment notice sent out in early January. Under property description, you'll see the address, lot number, block number, plan number, district lot, and PID number. B.C. Assessment stores information on all properties, and the legal description is also printed on the water installation order at the archives.

Another tool that you can try from home is VanMap at www.city.vancouver.bc.ca/vanmap/. Click on "Start Vanmap." Do an address search, and when the map comes up showing the neighbourhood of the house you're researching, click on the address of the house. Some of the information you can glean is the legal description and the assessed value.

If you're searching between January 2 and March 15, B.C. Assessment has an online service at bcassessment.bc.ca where you can look up your legal description and, if you're curious, snoop on everybody else's. You can find out helpful things such as what your neighbour's property just sold for and who has the most expensive house on the block. Click on "Assessments by Address," and after you agree to their "Terms of Use agreement," a box will pop up where you enter your address. You'll then see your house and its assessed value, as well as those of your neighbours. Next, click on "Sales Select System," and enter the area of your choice. A list of recent house sales in your immediate neighbourhood will appear. This service is only available for a short time during the property assessment appeal period. If you are researching many different houses, it is worth paying for a subscription to the BC OnLine, so you can access the service year round.

THE ARCHIVES

At this point, you've probably done as much as you can by yourself. Now it's time to visit the archives. The good news is that you can leave your inhaler at home. Archives are not the dusty, windowless places the name suggests, but treasure troves of information and great sources of old photos. The staff members are extremely knowledgeable and more than willing to help. And as an added bonus, the parking is free. Outside Vancouver, the Delta Museum and Archives is in a lovely heritage building and has recreated some of the area's early history. The New Westminster Museum and Archives is next to Irving House, reputed to be the oldest house in the Lower Mainland. North Vancouver Museum and Archives recently moved to a heritage building in Lynn Valley. Surrey Archives has fancy new digs at the 1912 Municipal Hall, the West Vancouver Museum and Archives is in one of the area's oldest heritage houses, and the City of Vancouver Archives is in an open and airy building close to the Vancouver Museum and H.R. MacMillan Space Centre. One warning though, when you enter one of these places, you go into a sort of time warp. Drop in for thirty minutes, emerge five hours later.

WATER RECORDS

If you still don't know the date your house was built, then it's time to hit the water service records. The CVA has water records on file from 1881 to 1991. Go to the filing drawer MCR 21 and find the card with your address. Take the card to the microfilm reader and note down the application number. I'd suggest taking copies of all the records relating to your house in case you need to refer back to something later. There is a printer attached to the microfilm reader. Go back to the filing cabinet and you'll find another drawer of microfilm filed by application number. Take this back to the microfilm reader. These installation orders are filed by date order. Find the installation order that corresponds to your address and this will give you the date of application, the legal description of the property, the owner or builder's name, and sometimes a few details such as the number of stories or even the building's use.

Keep in mind that while the date on the water installation order is likely the same year as the house was built, it's not definitive because sometimes the owner had a private source of water and didn't have service connected until years after the actual date of construction. In some cases, it might refer to a building long since demolished, but it's a good place to start. It's not a bad idea to take a look at the city directories and check back a few years to see if the house was occupied before this date.

Another catch is that before 1929, South Vancouver to the east of Cambie Street and Point Grey to the west of Cambie Street were separate municipalities. If you are researching a house built before 1929, and it is in one of these two areas, the information is filed under those areas.

If you live in Vancouver, you can also check with the engineering department at City Hall.

BUILDING PERMIT REGISTERS

Once you have the construction date, you can look in the city's building permit register. These run from 1901 to 1947 with an unfortunate gap in years from 1905 to 1908. These records are quite handy and give information on the date of the building permit application, the applicant's name (usually the owner or contractor), an architect if there was one, the value and the type of building, and how much it cost to build. For instance, in 1921, architect Bernard Palmer applied for a five hundred dollar garage at a house at 1146 Broughton, while Kwang Lei applied for a pig roaster for his house at 130 Keefer Street.

You'll need to use the blue binders in the bookcase against the wall to find out when your house was built. It's definitely not straightforward, as you have to start a few months before you think the house was built. Once you find the date, the records will be either on micro-film or in the original ledger. To look at it, you'll need to fill out a requisition form. These are huge, heavy, and delicate books, and you need to go through line by line of handwriting to find your address. In Vancouver, you can also get a copy of a building permit by visiting the property information counter of the data resource centre, community services group, on the second floor east wing of City Hall. You can have copies of up to three permits for the same property made for a small fee.

PROPERTY ASSESSMENT INFORMATION

Since you already have the application number and legal description from the water service installation card, it is also useful to get property tax assessment information. It's useful, but not easy. As with the building permit registers, the tax assessments come in both microfilm and the original ledgers. You need to go to the blue binders and find the "Property Tax Assessment Finding Aid" to get the location number. Use the date from the water installation, the block number, and the lot number to find the location in the binder. If you need to see the ledger, you must fill out a requisition form and hand it to one of the staffers.

The property assessment records are available from 1887 to 1890 and 1928 to 1977. They record the owner's name, and the value of the lot, the house, and any improvements to the property. They are also another source for sniffing out past property owners and land values. After 1977, you'll need to take a trip to the property tax branch at City Hall or, for current property tax assessment information, to the B.C. Assessment Authority.

GIVING YOUR HOUSE SOME CONTEXT

Now you know the age of your house, it wouldn't hurt to give it some context. In Vancouver, you can do a quick check on the history of your neighbourhood through www.city.vancouver.bc.ca/community_profiles/communitylist.htm. Also see the bibliography at the back of this book for a list of resources by historians such as Chuck Davis, Michael Kluckner, Bruce Macdonald, and John Atkin who have extensively researched different areas in the Lower Mainland and beyond.

PHOTOGRAPHS

There are literally thousands of historical photos available through the Vancouver Public Library, City of Vancouver Archives, various municipal archives, and the B.C. Archives. If you're lucky, you may find one or more of your own house or at least your street or immediate neighbourhood to add to the context of your search. Even better, many of these photographs are now available online. Check under the name of the house or apartment building, street, even the name of the previous owner. It's also worth checking nearby parks, commercial buildings, churches, hotels, schools, landmarks. Often this can turn up a photo of your house or others on the street.

FIRE INSURANCE MAPS

You can find fire insurance maps at the archives. Start with the ones around the year your house was built. These maps were drawn up for insurance purposes and show the type of construction, the number of stories, the positioning of the building on the lot and driveways. Take a careful look at the outline of your house. You might discover that it once had a full-length verandah or a long since demolished garage that explains those slabs of concrete in the back yard.

If you can't find your building, the street name and/or number may have changed over the years, especially if your house was built before 1929 when South Vancouver and Point Grey were separate municipalities. After the merge, many street names became numbers or just changed names for no obvious reason. Fortunately, Elizabeth Walker did copious research, which culminated in her book *Street Names of Vancouver* published by the Vancouver Historical Society in 1999. The archives and the library have a copy.

ARCHITECTURAL PLANS

If you have a house designed by Charles Van Norman, Ross A. Lort, or another prominent architect, you could be in luck. At the City of Vancouver Archives, architectural drawings are found through a card index searchable by the address or the architect's name. These drawings show the original floor plan, the elevation, structural specifications, additions or alterations, as well as interior and exterior ornamentation.

The City of Vancouver also carries architectural plans, but you will either need to be the owner or have the owner's written permission to look at these. There is a fee to access the plans (twenty-six dollars at the time of my research), and each copy is eight dollars. See the Property Information Counter, second floor, east wing City Hall.

LAND TITLE SEARCH

If you are trying to get a heritage designation for your house, you'll need to do an actual title search. Also, if you are flush with cash and short on time, grab the legal description (lot and plan number) of your property and get on your computer. The website ltsa.ca will give you all the information and costs you need to know, but they strongly suggest that you hire a professional to do it for you. You can find these title search companies or registry agencies in the directory. They have direct access to records in the Victoria, New Westminster (covers Vancouver), and Kamloops Land Title Offices and tend to charge between seventy and ninety dollars an hour plus applicable taxes and any photocopying charges for historical research. You'll be able to find out not only who bought and sold the property, but the purchase price, any mortgages held on the title, and bankruptcies. They could also turn up such treasures as wills or death certificates in the course of their search. An average search will run you a couple of hundred bucks, but the costs can really ratchet up quickly depending on things like how many times your property has changed hands (could be anywhere from a couple to a hundred transactions and there's a charge for each one), whether it was subdivided, and how much information you can give them before they start.

Title searches go right back to who first owned the land. If you want to save some money and you know your house was built in 1920, then have the researcher stop there. You can also have them focus the search on a particular time period or on a certain family name. Or you can give them a budget and ask them to check in with you if and when they hit that magic number.

The actual Land Titles office will also do a historical search of your land title for a fee, but these searches are just of the land—not the actual buildings, and can take up to three months.

WHO LIVED IN YOUR HOUSE?
THE DIRECTORIES

If you've searched through land titles, you know who owned the house but not necessarily who lived in it. That's the time to hit the city directories. These are available on microfilm at the Vancouver Public Library, seventh floor. For those of us who have an aversion to microfilm, the City of Vancouver Archives has a full set, mostly original. They are showing their age and require great care. It's worth checking into your local archives if you're outside Vancouver. New Westminster Public Library has a set of directories, for example, as does the West Vancouver Museum and Archives. The North Vancouver Archives has most of the directories from 1925.

In case you are new to microfiche or microfilm, it's probably worth me mentioning that these are sheets or reels of film that reproduce all sorts of historical information. Using them requires patience; searching through a month's worth of newspaper articles can make you crazy. But when you find what you're looking for, or stumble over something you weren't, it's like winning the lottery.

The city directories date from around 1860 until the last year it came out in 1996.

Now that you've got a good idea when your house was built, look up your address in the directory for that year. With any luck, the name of a past resident will pop up. Look up his name—and it will be "his" until about 1934, when married women first rate a mention—and chances are good that you'll get that person's occupation. Go back a couple of years, just in case residents are listed before the water connection. They may have had a well. Then, because you want to know everything about this person—what they did, whether they changed jobs, how long they lived at your house—you'll need to go through every year. Make sure you get any initials and the name of the wife, because this will come in handy when you start to search vital statistics, census information, and obituaries later.

James Johnstone, a Vancouver home researcher offers this advice. "If you are searching houses in the 1910s and 1920s, the decade before wives names were included, it's sometimes useful to grab the 1936 or 1937 directory to see if the same name is listed with a spouse's name. Divorces happen and first spouses die in childbirth, but more often than not you can assume that the spouse's name goes back to when the husband's first appeared at the address." Johnstone suggests cross-checking this information with the B.C. Archives marriage records.

It can be really infuriating if you're searching for a Chinese or Japanese resident, as often, in the early days, they are just listed as "oriental" or "foreigner." As well, spelling wasn't considered particularly important, so it's worth trying a couple of variations. If you can't find it under Smith, try Smythe, Smithe, etc. The directories also list the resident, which is not necessarily the owner. Some years have an asterisk which indicates the actual owner, but this feature is not used consistently. If you need to know the actual owner and the dates the property was sold, then you have to do a title search.

"Another thing to remember is that some non-British names were spelled in various ways over the course of the years," says Johnstone. "Listings that initially don't seem to be related sometimes end up being the same person. For example, a listing from 712 Hawks of Derto Rose and later Ross Dorigo, ended up really being Rosario De Rico."

If you can't find your address, double check in Elizabeth Walker's *Street Names of Vancouver* that the street name or number hasn't changed. And just when you start getting used to the format of a city directory, it can change. Sometimes all the areas of Greater Vancouver are listed together, especially in the earlier years. In other years, New Westminster, Burnaby, North and West Vancouver are broken out from the rest of the directory. In some years, numbered streets may be with the numbers or may be spelled out in the alphabetical list of street names. Sometimes the numbered streets are at the front, sometimes at the back.

If your house was built between, say, 1904 and 1913, the owner may never have lived in the house. There was an awful lot of money made in real-estate speculation during this period, and a number of houses were left vacant after the bust, some due to high mortgages on now worthless lots (a pattern that seems to repeat itself through history). In fact, the price of land didn't recover to pre-bust levels for another forty years.

Another reason you might find years of vacancies at your address is, of course, because of World War One. Your past owner/resident could have been one of the thirty thousand Vancouver men who fought in the war and may have died. Veterans Affairs Canada has a list of all those who died fighting for Canada in a variety of wars. Go to http://www.vac-acc.gc.ca/ then click on "Canada Remembers" at the top right of the page. Next, click on "The Books of Remembrance" tab on the navigation bar to the left. Click on the "Books of Remembrance" tab on the new page, and it will take you through to the various wars.

MORE ABOUT THE PEOPLE WHO ONCE LIVED IN YOUR HOUSE

Now that you have their names, you can check out a few online sources to flesh out your profile. Go to bcarchives.gov.bc.ca and click on "Vital Events." Here you'll find information on births (1872–1903), marriages (1872–1931), colonial marriages (1859-1872), deaths (1872-1986), and baptisms over the past 120 twenty years. Historical marriage registrations may show the age and birth place of the bride and groom, information about their parents, the occupation of the bride and groom, and the signatures of the couple and the witnesses. Death registrations may contain the person's occupation and cause of death. You may need to get detailed information from the Vancouver Public Library's Fine Arts and History department. Jot down the microfilm number and look for the corresponding microfilm reel. You'll discover things like occupation, date of birth, father's and mother's names, cause of death, whether an autopsy was done and whether the death was through "accident or violence." The birth record gives you the father's name and occupation, which can be handy for making historical connections later.

You can also find the Vital Events information on microfilms at the B.C. Archives and at the Cloverdale branch of the Surrey Public Library. The Surrey Public Library has one of the best genealogical collections in the province.

CENSUS

Finding information through the census will give you a whole new appreciation for why it's important to cheerfully slog through them every five years, tick the box giving your descendants permission to get this information about you, and not lie. 1901 is the last year for which information is complete and available to the public. Then there is no information until 1911, and it is still a work in progress. While you might think this is no help if your house wasn't built until say 1915, if the person you are researching was born in 1901, it can provide a bunch of information, including their age and next of kin. Check out the census online at automatedgenealogy.com. It gives you the people in the household, their relationship to each other, marital status, and their date of birth. There's also a form where you can register with other people who are interested in a particular individual—and possibly find tons more information.

For even more information, including occupation, annual earnings, country of birth, year of immigration, and religion you'll need to head to the Surrey Public Library, the University of B.C., Simon Fraser University, or the Vancouver Public Library where you'll find detailed census information in Fine Arts and History on level six.

Newspaper Articles

Newspaper articles can be one of your best sources of information. The Vancouver Public Library, level five, keeps full copies of *The Vancouver Sun, The Province, Vancouver Courier,* and other local newspapers dating from the 1880s on microfilm. Find defunct newspapers at Special Collections on level seven. Here you'll also find helpful indexes to a variety of different subjects available on microfilm to aid in your search.

It's also worth plugging the person you are researching, or even the address, into the library's free database, accessible with your library card number. This gives you access to Canadian Newsstand and the full text of ninety-four B.C. newspapers and other major Canadian dailies dating back to 1985. I found many articles that mentioned long dead people, letters to the editor from and detailed interviews with people I was researching, and obituaries full of information about their relatives.

Newspaper Clipping Files

If your house or person is well known, it's worth searching through the clippings file. It's also a great way to avoid microfilm. Most of the clipping files are in the filing cabinets in front of the information desk on level five of the main branch of the Vancouver Public Library. Some, like the crime files, are kept behind the desk. You can search through the index first at www.vpl.ca. Go to the home page and click on "Electronic Resources." Scroll down until you reach the newspaper clipping index.

New Westminster Museum and Archives also collects people files on many of its residents.

OTHER SOURCES

SPECIAL DIRECTORIES

As well as the city directories, it's worth checking out some other sources, including professional association directories, business and industry directories, and ethnic directories. There's even something called the Vancouver Social Registry and the Elite Directory of Vancouver that contain wonderful information such as the day you can drop by to someone's manor for a visit, and the names of the members of the Vancouver Club, the Vancouver Hunting Club, the Vancouver Riding Club and the Vancouver Rowing Club.

A typical 1914 entry reads:

Nichol, Mr. and Mrs. W.C.

Shaughnessy Heights Bay 2390

Receives Wednesdays.

VOTERS' LISTS

Voters' lists are tricky, and I'd use them only as a last resort. They do give names and information on occupations and street of residence, but you have to know the proper electoral district to get you there. And you can't see lists from the past twenty-five years. Also, if you are looking for someone of First Nations, Chinese, Japanese, or South East Asian descent, you are out of luck, unless you are looking at records that are "post-1948", the year they were given the right to vote.

MAJOR MATTHEWS FILES

Major Matthews, Vancouver's first archivist, is a hero to modern researchers for all the work he accumulated throughout his long life. He amassed a huge amount of information from interviews with the city's pioneers. The Early Vancouver Volumes are an abundant source of information. Search for your subject through an amalgamated index that you'll find on the reference shelf. The index will lead you to ledgers full of handwritten interviews between Major Matthews and various pioneers that offer up fascinating anecdotes and candid conversations.

Also check your subject's name on the City of Vancouver Archives' online database for Major Matthews Topical Files. If you are lucky, you'll get a reference to a microfilm card and all sorts of information, ranging from newspaper articles to invitations and biographies.

NORTHWEST HISTORY AT VANCOUVER PUBLIC LIBRARY

Housed amid Special Collections on the seventh floor, this section specializes in the history of B.C. and the Northwest Coast, especially before 1976. You can find information on houses and buildings in Vancouver and the Lower Mainland in the form of books, pamphlets and magazines. It's also available on handy, old-fashioned alphabetical card files.

DEATH

Death records are a wonderful thing when it comes to historical research. As well as the information you've found through vital statistics and a trip to view the death certificate at the library, the B.C. Archives has coroner's inquests on file from 1859 to 1967. These investigations rule on cause of death and often contain witness statements, transcripts, and autopsy reports and findings. The catch is, if you are looking for records created after 1910, your request has to be reviewed by the information and privacy section of the B.C. Archives which can take thirty days or more. More accessible, and available on microfilm, are probated wills between 1861 and 1981. To access these, you need the date the will was filed, not the year of death. It's worth the hunt. Wills and other estate papers offer up volumes of valuable information about the ownership and contents of a house and the nearest and dearest.

Burial Records are another source of information for the name, age, birthplace, burial date, cause of death, and, often, next of kin. And more and more funeral homes and cemeteries are posting these records and tombstone inscriptions online. Mountain View Cemetery has a record of the date and location of the grave on microfilm at the City of Vancouver Archives via the health department binder under "Public Record Finding Aids." A typical entry gives the date of burial, cause of death, name of doctor, religion, and the cost for the lot and digging the grave. The City of Vancouver Archives also has tombstone inscriptions from 1887-1983.

If you're searching locations of graves, also try the Mountain View website at http://www.city.vancouver.bc.ca/commsvcs/nonmarketoperations/mountainview/burials/burials.htm. Much of the information from the binders is transcribed here and it's a helpful tool for finding spouses names that not listed in the directories before the 1930s.

In New Westminster, Bowell's Funeral Home has a record of deaths that occurred between 1932 and 1956 and is adding to it all the time. It gives the date of birth, the marital status and spouse's name, the occupation, the place of birth, parents' names and places of birth, place and location of the grave, and cause of death. Copies of Bowell's

record are available through the New Westminster Heritage page at nwheritage.org/her-
itagesite/genealogy/index.htm.

Obituaries are another excellent source of information. At the City of Vancouver
Archives, Major Matthews has gathered local obits from 1931 to 1943. Also, check newspapers at the Vancouver Public Library around the date of death. The New Westminster
Museum and Archives has a card file index of obituary notices that appear in the local
newspapers, the *British Columbian* and the *Mainland Guardian*. This index covers the
period 1861 to 1940, is filed alphabetically by surname, and provides a reference to the
newspaper, date, and page number on which the obit appears. These items are often full
of names of surviving friends and relatives that you can track down to find out more
information.

ORAL HISTORIES

Oral histories are an often overlooked source of information. Talk to your neighbours,
relatives and friends of past owners, senior citizens in the area, people at history associations, and local history buffs. It's worth a visit to your local archives to get names of local
researchers. When you find someone, make sure to give yourself lots of time, take a tape
recorder, and listen carefully.

LOCAL RESOURCES

B.C. Archives
675 Belleville Street
Victoria, BC V8W 9W2
(250) 387-1952
bcarchives.gov.bc.ca

B.C. Assessment Authority
1537 Hillside Ave.
Victoria, BC V8T 4Y2
(250) 595-6211 or
Toll Free: 1-800-661-1780
bcassessment.bc.ca

City of Vancouver
453 West 12th Avenue
Vancouver, BC V5Y 1V4
Building Permit information:
(604) 873-7537
Engineering department
(water connection) (604) 873-7644
city.vancouver.bc.ca

City of Vancouver Archives
1150 Chestnut Street
Vancouver, BC V6J 3J9
(604) 736-8561
city.vancouver.bc.ca/archives

Heritage Society of B.C.
914 Garthland Place West
Victoria, BC V9A 4J5
(250) 384-4840

Land Titles Office
(Vancouver and New Westminster)
88 6th Street
New Westminster, BC V3L 5B3
(604) 660-2595

New Westminster Public Library
716 6th Avenue
New Westminster, BC V3M 2B3
(604) 527-4660
nwpl.ca and nwheritage.org

University of B.C. Special Collections
Main library, 1956 Main Mall,
Vancouver, BC V6T 1Z4
(604) 822-2521
library.ubc.ca/spcoll/index.html

Vancouver Heritage Foundation
402-510 West Hastings Street
Vancouver, BC V6B 1L8
(604) 254-9411
vancouverheritagefoundation.org

Vancouver Historical Society
P.O. Box 3071
Vancouver, B.C. V6B 3X6
(604) 878-9140
vancouver-historical-society.ca

Vancouver Public Library
350 West Georgia Street
Vancouver, BC V6B 6B1
(604) 331 3782
Photo orders (604) 331-3776
http://www3.vpl.vancouver.bc.ca/spe/
histphotos/

BIBLIOGRAPHY

Atkin, John. (1994). *Strathcona: Vancouver's First Neighbourhood*. Vancouver: Whitecap Books.

Atkin, John & Kluckner, Michael (2005). *Vancouver Walks: Discovering City Heritage*. Vancouver: Stellar Press.

Bagley, Clarence B (1929). *History of King County, Washington*. Chicago: S.J. Clarke Publishing Co.

Bell-Irving, Elizabeth (1988). *Crofton House School. The first 90 Years 1898-1988*. Vancouver: Crofton House School.

Bingham, Janet (1985). *Samuel Maclure Architect*. Canada: Horsdal and Schubart.

Bingham, Janet (1996). *More Than a House: The Story of Roedde House and Barclay Heritage Square*. Vancouver: Roedde House Preservation Society.

Border, Martha & Sparks, Dawn (1989). *Echoes Across the Inlet*. Vancouver: Deep Cove and Area Heritage Association.

Chong, Denise (1997). *The Concubine's Children*. Toronto: Penguin Books.

Choy, Wayson (1995). *The Jade Peony*. Vancouver: Douglas & McIntyre.

Choy, Wayson (1999). *Paper Shadows: A Chinatown Childhood*. Toronto: Viking Penguin Books.

Culos, Raymond (1998). *Vancouver's Society of Italians*. Sechelt: Harbour Publishing.

Davis, Chuck, (Ed.) (1997). *The Greater Vancouver Book*. Surrey: The Linkman Press.

Francis, Daniel (2004). *Mayor Louis Taylor and the Rise of Vancouver*. Vancouver: Arsenal Pulp Press.

Francis, Daniel, (Ed.) (2000). *Encyclopedia of British Columbia*. Sechelt: Harbour Publishing.

Hayes, Derek (2005). *Historical Atlas of Vancouver and the Lower Fraser Valley*. Vancouver: Douglas and McIntyre.

Itter, Carole & Marlatt, Daphne (1979). *Opening Doors: Vancouver's East End*. Vancouver: Sound Heritage Series, Vol. VII, nos. 1-2. Victoria: aural History Program.

Johnstone, James. Home history for Bill Richardson, 808 Dunlevy Street.

Kalman, Harold, Phillips, Ron & Ward, Robin (1993). *Exploring Vancouver: The Essential Architectural Guide*. Vancouver: University of British Columbia Press.

Kells, Kay (1974). *A Brief History of Port Kells*. Reprint: Fraser Valley Regional Library.

Kluckner, Michael (1984). *Vancouver the Way it Was*. Vancouver: Whitecap Books.

Kluckner, Michael (2005). *Vanishing British Columbia*. Vancouver: University of British Columbia Press.

Kluckner, Michael (1987). *M.I. Rogers: 1869-1965*. Privately printed.

Kogawa, Joy (1981). *Obasan*. Toronto: Penguin Canada.

Lawrence, Sharon (2004). *Jimi Hendrix, the Man, the Magic, the Truth*. Toronto: Harper Entertainment.

Luxton, Donald, (Ed.) (2003). *Building the West: The Early Architects of British Columbia*. Vancouver: Talon.

Macdonald, Ian & O'Keefe, Betty (1997). *The Mulligan Affair: Top Cop on the Take*. Victoria: Heritage House Publishing Company.

Macdonald, Ian & O'Keefe, Betty (2000). *A Story of Clans, Tongs, Murder and Bigotry*. Victoria: Heritage House Publishing Company.

Macdonald, Ian & O'Keefe, Betty (2001). *Merchant Prince: The Story of Alexander Duncan McRae.* Victoria: Heritage House.

MacGill, Elsie Gregory (1955). *My Mother the Judge.* Toronto: The Ryerson Press.

McDonald, Glen & Kirkwood, John (1985). *How Come I'm Dead?* Surrey: Hancock House.

McNicoll, Susan (2003). *British Columbia Murders: Mysteries, Crimes and Scandals,* Amazing Stories. Canmore: Altitude Publishing.

Moore, Vincent (1981). *Gladiator of the Courts: Angelo Branca.* Vancouver: Douglas and McIntyre.

Newman, Peter C. (1998). *Titans: How the New Canadian Establishment Seized Power.* Toronto: Viking.

Newman, Peter C. (1978). *The Bronfman Dynasty.* Toronto: McClelland and Stewart.

Nicol, Eric (1978). *Vancouver.* Toronto: Doubleday Canada.

Petrie, Blair (1995). *Mole Hill Living Heritage.* Vancouver: Living Heritage Society.

Scholefield and Moway (1914). *British Columbia from the Earliest Times to the Present.* Vancouver: S.J. Clarke Publishing Company.

Scott, Jack David (1985). *Once in the Royal City: The Heritage of New Westminster.* Vancouver: Whitecap Books.

Snyders, Tom (2001). *Namely Vancouver: A Hidden History of Vancouver Place Names.* Vancouver: Arsenal Pulp Press.

Starkins, Edward (1984). *Who Killed Janet Smith?* Toronto: MacMillan Canada.

Stone, Jim (2002). *My Dad the Rum Runner.* Waterloo: North Waterloo Academic Press.

Swan, Joe (1986) *A Century of Service: The Vancouver Police 1886-1986.* Vancouver: Vancouver Police Historical Society and Centennial Museum.

Swan, Joe (1987). *The Police Murders: True Stories from the Vancouver Police Archives.* Vancouver: West Ender Books.

Walker, Elizabeth (1999). *Street Names of Vancouver.* Vancouver: Vancouver Historical Society.

Watt, Robert D. (1980). *Rainbows in Our Walls: Art and Stained Glass in Vancouver.* Vancouver: Vancouver Centennial Museum.

Webster, Jack (1990). *Webster!* Vancouver: Douglas and McIntyre.

Williams, David Ricardo (1986). *Mayor Gerry: The Remarkable Gerald Grattan McGreer.* Vancouver: Douglas and McIntyre.

Willoughby, Malcolm Francis. *Rum War at Sea.* U.S. Government Printing Office.

Wilson, Ethel (1949). *The Innocent Traveller.* Toronto: MacMillan Canada.

Wolf, Jim (2005). *Royal City: A Photographic History of New Westminster, 1858 to 1960.* Victoria: Heritage House.

Yee, Paul (2006). *Saltwater City: An Illustrated History of the Chinese in Vancouver.* Vancouver: Douglas and McIntyre.

NEWSPAPERS:

Burnaby Now, Coquitlam Now, Delta Optimist, Kingston Whig Standard, North Shore News, The Ottawa Citizen, The Province, Surrey Leader, Vancouver Courier, The Vancouver Sun

INDEX

188